www.EZmethods.com

EZ SOLUTIONS

TEST PREP SERIES

GENERAL

TEST TAKER'S MANUAL

EZ SIMPLIFIED SOLUTIONS – THE BREAKTHROUGH IN TEST PREP!

LEADERS IN TEST PREP SOLUTIONS – WE MAKE IT EZ FOR YOU!

AUTHOR: PUNIT RAJA SURYACHANDRA

EZ Solutions
P O Box 10755
Silver Spring, MD 20914
USA

EZ SOLUTIONS
P.O. Box 10755
Silver Spring, MD 20914
USA

Conceived, conceptualized, written, and edited by:
Punit Raja SuryaChandra, EZ Solutions

PRINTED AND MANUFACTURED IN THE UNITED STATES OF AMERICA

TABLE OF CONTENTS

PREFACE

HIGHLIGHTS:
- About EZ Solutions
- About Our Author
- About EZ Books
- About This Book

▪ ABOUT EZ SOLUTIONS

EZ Solutions – the breakthrough in test-preparation!

EZ Solutions is an organization formed to provide *simplified solutions* for test-preparation and tutoring. Although EZ Solutions is a fairly new name in the publishing industry, it has quickly become a respected publisher of test-prep books, study guides, study aids, handbooks, and other reference works. EZ publications and educational materials are highly respected, and they continue to receive an unprecedented amount of praise from professionals, instructors, librarians, parents, and students.

OBJECTIVE: Our ultimate objective is to help you *achieve academic and scholastic excellence*. We possess the right blend and matrix of skills and expertise that are required to not only do justice to our programs and publications, but also to handle them most effectively and efficiently. We are confident that our state-of-the-art programs/publications will give you a completely *new dimension* by enhancing your skill set and improving your overall performance.

MISSION: Our mission is to foster continuous knowledge to develop and enhance each student's skills through innovative and methodical programs/publications coupled with our add-on services – leading to a *better career and life* for our students.

OUR PHILOSOPHY: We subscribe to the traditional philosophy that everyone is equally capable of learning and that the natural, though sometimes unfulfilled and unexplored impetus of people is towards growth and development. We know that the human brain is undoubtedly a very powerful and efficient problem-solving tool, and every individual is much more capable than they realize. We strive to implement this philosophy throughout our books by helping our students explore their *potential* so that they can *perform at their optimum level*.

OUR COMMITMENT TOWARDS YOUR SATISFACTION: Reinventing, Redesigning, and Redefining Success: We are committed to providing *total customer satisfaction* that exceeds your expectations! Your satisfaction is extremely important to us, and your approval is one of the most important indicators that we have done our job correctly.

Long-Term Alliance: We, at EZ, look forward to forming a *long-term alliance* with all our readers who buy our book(s), for the days, months, and years to come. Moreover, our commitment to client service is one of our most important and distinguished characteristics. We also encourage our readers to contact us for any further assistance, feedback, suggestions, or inquiries.

EZ Solutions publishing series include books for the following major standardized tests:
- GMAT
- SAT
- PSAT
- ASVAB
- PRAXIS Series
- GRE
- ACT
- CLEP
- TOEFL
- Other (national and state) Standardized Tests

EZ Solutions aims to provide good quality study aids in a wide variety of disciplines to the following:
Students who have not yet completed high school
High School students preparing to enter college
College students preparing to enter graduate or post-graduate school
Anyone else who is simply looking to improve their skills
Students from every walk of life, of any background, at any level, in any field, with any ambition, can find what they are looking for among EZ Solutions' publications.

FOREIGN STUDENTS: All of our books are designed, keeping in mind the unique needs of students from North and South America, U.K., Europe, Middle East, Far East, and Asia. Foreign students from countries around the world seeking to obtain education in the United States will find the assistance they need in EZ Solutions' publications.

CONTACT US: Feel free to contact us, and one of our friendly specialists will be more than happy to assist you with your queries, or feel free to browse through our website for lots of useful information.
E-Mail: info@EZmethods.com
Phone: (301) 622-9597
Mail: EZ Solutions, P.O. Box 10755, Silver Spring, MD 20914, USA
Website: www.EZmethods.com

FEEDBACK: The staff of EZ Solutions hopes that you find our books helpful and easy to use. If you have any specific suggestions, comments, or feedback, please email us at: feedback@EZmethods.com

BUSINESS DEVELOPMENT: If you are interested in exploring business development opportunities, including forming a partnership alliance with us, kindly email us at: partners@EZmethods.com.

PRODUCT REGISTRATION: In order to get the most up-to-date information about this and our other books, you must register your purchase with EZ solutions by emailing us at: products@EZmethods.com, or by visiting our website www.EZmethods.com.

ERRORS AND INACCURACIES: We are not responsible for any typographical errors or inaccuracies contained in this publication. The information, prices, and discounts given in this book are subject to change without prior notice. To report any kind of errors or inaccuracies in this publication, kindly email us at: errors@EZmethods.com.

▪ABOUT OUR AUTHOR

The name of the man behind EZ publication series is **Punit Raja SuryaChandra**, who is also the founder of our company. He holds a Bachelors in Business and an MBA. It took him many years to write and publish these unique books. He researched every single book available in the market for test-preparation, and actually realized there is not even one book that is truly complete with all the content and concepts. This was the single most important reason that prompted him to write these books, and hence our **EZ prep guidebooks were born**. He has made every effort to make these books as comprehensive and as complete as possible. His expertise and experience are as diverse as the subjects that are represented in our books. He has the breadth and depth of experience required to write books of this magnitude and intensity. Without his unparalleled and unmatched skills and determination, none of this would have been possible.

In developing these books, his primary goal has been to give everyone the same advantages as the students we tutor privately or students who take our classes. Our tutoring and classroom solutions are only available to a limited number of students; however, with these books, any student in any corner of the world can benefit the same level of service at a fraction of the cost. Therefore, you should take this book as your personal EZ tutor or instructor, because that's precisely how it has been designed.

ACKNOWLEDGEMENTS:
Our author would like to extend his vote of appreciation and gratitude to all his family members for their unconditional and continuous support, to all his close friends for their trust and confidence in him, and to all his colleagues for their helpful consultation and generous advice.

Our EZ books have benefited from dedicated efforts and labors of our author and other members of the editorial staff. Here at EZ, we all wish you the best as you get comfortable, and settle down with your EZ tutor to start working on preparing for your test. In pursuing an educational dream, you have a wonderful and an exciting opportunity ahead of you. All of us at EZ Solutions wish you the very best!

▪ABOUT EZ BOOKS

THE EZ NAME:
All our books have been written in a very easy to read manner, and in a very easy to understand fashion, so that students of any background, of any aptitude, of any capacity, of any skill-set, of any level, can benefit from them. These books are not specifically written for the **dummies** or for the **geniuses**; instead, they are written for students who fit into any category of intellectual acumen. This is how we acquired the name **"EZ Solutions"** for our publications – and as the name itself suggests, **we make everything EZ for you**!

THE EZ TUTOR:
Like any good tutor, EZ Tutor will work with you **individually and privately**, providing you with all the tools needed to improve your testing skills. It will assist you in recognizing your weaknesses, and enlighten you on how to improve upon them while transforming them into strengths. Of course, it will also point out your strengths as well, so that you can make them even stronger. By employing innovative techniques, EZ tutor will **stimulate, activate, and accelerate your learning process**. Soon after you start working with your EZ tutor, you will see **remarkable and noticeable improvement** in your performance by utilizing your newly acquired learning skills.

Whenever, Wherever, and However: EZ tutor also has the **flexibility** to work with you whenever you like – day or night, wherever you like – indoors or outdoors, and however you like – for as long or as short. While working with your EZ tutor, you can work at your own pace, you can go as fast or as slow as you like, repeat sections as many times as you need, and skip over sections you already know well. Your EZ tutor will also give you explanations, not just correct answers, and it will be **infinitely patient and adaptable**. Hence, our EZ Tutor will make you a more intelligent and smarter test-taker, and will help you maximize your score!

ADD-ON OPTIONS: Turn your EZ Virtual Tutor into a Real Tutor!

EZ TUTORING OVER THE PHONE:
Along with buying the entire series of our modules, students can also add on services like email/online support and/or telephone support. In fact, you can get the best preparation for your test by blending our professional 1-on-1 tutoring with our state-of-the-art books. The most important feature of our add-on features is our individualized and personalized approach that works toward building your self-confidence, and enhancing your ability to learn and perform better. This will also invigorate your motivational, organizational, as well as your learning skills. Our phone specialists are highly qualified, experienced, innovative, and well trained. You can do all this in the exclusivity and comfort of your home. Students can get in touch with one of our specialists anytime they need help – we'll be there for you, whenever you need us! We offer several packages with different levels, features, and customizations for tutoring over the phone to suit your individualized needs. Contact us for more details.

EZ 1-ON-1 TEST-TAKING & ADMISSION CONSULTATION:
We understand that standardized tests and school/college admissions can sometimes become very stressful. Our 1-on-1 Test-Taking & Admission Consulting Program can dramatically reduce your stress and anxiety. One of our consultants can personally guide you through the entire process, starting from familiarizing you with a test to getting you successfully admitted into a school/college of your choice. Again, you can do all this in the exclusivity and comfort of your home. We offer several packages with different levels, features, and customizations for test-taking and admission consultation over the phone to suit your individualized needs. Contact us for more details.
The following are some of the features of our EZ 1-on-1 Test-Taking & Admission Consulting Program:
- Familiarize you with a particular test.
- Equip you with test-taking skills for each section of your test.
- Reduce test-taking anxiety, stress, nervousness, and test-fever with personal counseling.
- Draft and edit your essays.
- Re-design your resume.
- Prepare you for a telephone or personal interview.
- Select the right school/college & help with admission application procedures.
- Presentation Skills – how to present and market yourself.

EZ UNIQUE FEATURES:

Your EZ Tutor offers you the following unique features that will highlight important information, and will let you find them quickly as and when you need to review them.

EZ STRATEGIES: It provides you with many powerful, effective, proven, and time tested strategies for various concepts, and shows you exactly how to use them to attack different question types. Many of these test-taking strategies cannot be found in any other books!

EZ SHORTCUTS: It gives you many time-saving shortcuts you can apply to save yourself some very valuable testing-time while solving a question on your actual test.

EZ TACTICS: It shows you several important tactics to use so that you can solve problems in the smartest way.

EZ DEFINITIONS: It defines all the key definitions in an easy to understand manner so that you get a clear description and concise understanding of all the key terms.

EZ RULES: It presents all the important rules in an orderly manner so that you can learn the basic rules of all the concepts.

EZ STEPS: It walks you through hundreds of concepts, showing you how to tackle every question type in an organized user-friendly step-by-step easy-to-understand methodology that adapts to your understanding and needs so that you get the best procedural knowledge.

EZ MULTIPLE/ALTERNATE METHODS: It gives you a choice of multiple methods of answering the same question so that you can choose the method that seems easiest to you.

EZ SUMMARIES: It lists a complete summary of all the important concepts in an ordered and organized manner so that you will never have to hunt for them.

EZ FACTS: It provides you with numerous key facts about various principles so that you know all the facts-and-figures of the material you are reviewing.

EZ HINTS: It supplies you with innumerable hints and clues so that you can use them to become a smarter and wiser test-taker.

EZ TIPS: It also presents you with many tips and pointers that will prevent you from making any careless mistakes or falling into traps.

EZ NOTES: It reminds you to make notes of some important points that will come handy while answering a question.

EZ WARNINGS/CAUTIONS: It warns you of some obvious mistakes that will prevent you from making them while answering a question.

EZ EXCEPTIONS: It makes you aware of the exceptions and exclusions that apply to any particular rule.

EZ REFERENCES: It gives you references of related materials that you may want to refer to in other parts of the same or different modules, while learning a specific concept.

EZ SPOTS: It lists buzzwords and phrases that will help you easily spot some specific question types.

EZ PROBLEM SET-UP: It converts even some of the most complex problems into an easy to understand mathematical statement so that you understand accurately how to interpret the problems.

EZ PROBLEM EXPLANATIONS: It provides easy to understand explanations within square brackets for each step of the problem so that you know exactly what you need to do in each step.

EZ SOLVED EXAMPLES: It also throws several realistic solved examples with easy to understand detailed explanations for each and every question type explained so that you can understand and learn how to apply the concepts.

EZ PRACTICE EXERCISES: Last but not the least; it also includes intensive realistic practice exercises with easy to understand detailed explanations for each and every question type explained so that you can put to practice what you learned in an actual test question – solved examples will help you understand the concepts & practice will make you perfect!

GUESS WHAT!! No other book offers you so much. Your EZ tutor strives to provide you with the ***best possible training*** for your test, and ***best value for your time and money***; and it is infinitely committed to providing you with ***state-of-the-art*** material.

Advantages: Amazing results in the first few days of the program!

Disadvantages: Only if you don't make use of our programs and publications!

THE EZ ADVANTAGE:

EZ TEST-PREP PROGRAM BROKEN INTO MODULES:
Instead of having a ***big fat ugly scary all-in-one gigantic book***, we have broken our entire test-prep program into ***small easy-to-use modules***.
- **Exclusivity:** Each module is exclusively dedicated to covering one major content area in extensive depth and breadth, allowing you to master each topic by getting an in-depth review.
- **More Content:** You will find many more topics and many more pages per topic than what you can find in all other books combined.
- **Tailored and Customized:** Separated modules offer test-takers of all levels with a more tailored and customized approach towards building specific foundational and advanced skills, and successfully preparing for the test.

EZ TO READ, CARRY, AND MANAGE:
EZ Modules are convenient – they are ***easier to read, carry, and manage***.
- **EZ to Read:** EZ Modules are easier to read with text in spacious pages with a bigger font size than those other books with overcrowded pages with a small print.
- **EZ to Carry:** EZ Modules are easier to carry and hold than those other big fat bulky gigantic books.
- **EZ to Manage:** EZ Modules are overall easier to manage than those other all-in-one books.

BUY ONE MODULE OR THE ENTIRE SERIES:
The individually separated modules give you the flexibility to buy only those modules that cover the areas you think you need to work on; nevertheless, we strongly suggest you buy our entire series of modules. In fact, the most efficient and effective way to get the most out of our publications is to use our entire set of modules in conjunction with each other, and not just a few. Each module can be independently bought and studied; however, the modules are somehow connected with and complement the other modules. Therefore, if you are serious about getting a good score on your test, we sincerely recommend you purchase our entire series of modules. Contact us to order, or go to www.EZmethods.com, or check your local bookstore (look at the EZ Book Store on the last page for more information).

NO NEED TO REFER TO ANY OTHER BOOK:
Almost all other test-prep books contain a small disclaimer in some corner. They themselves spell it out very loud and clear, and admit that their book is only a brief review of some important topics; hence, it should not be considered to be an overall review of all the concepts. Most other test-preparation guides only include information for you to get familiar with the kind of topics that may appear on the test, and they suggest that you refer to additional textbooks, or consult other reference books if you want more detailed information and to get an in-depth knowledge of all the concepts. These books are not designed to be a one-stop book to learn everything you must know; instead, they are more like a

summary of some important points. Moreover, they assume that you already know everything, or at least most of the concepts.

However, if you are using our EZ modules to prepare for your test, it's the opposite case, you don't need to refer or consult any other book or text or any other source for assistance. On the contrary, we, in fact, discourage you from referring to any other book, just because there is absolutely no reason to. Our EZ modules contain everything that you need to know in order to do well on your test. We haven't left anything out, and we don't assume anything. Even if you don't know anything, you will find everything in our modules from topics that are frequently tested to topics that are rarely tested, and everything in between. The only topics that you won't find in our books are the topics that will probably never appear on your test!

Frequently Tested: Included in our review – topics that are repeatedly tested on your test, on a regularly basis
Occasionally Tested: Included in our review – topics that are sometimes tested on your test, every now and then
Rarely Tested: Included in our review – topics that are seldom tested on your test, very infrequently
Never Tested: Not included in our review – since these topics are never tested on your test, we don't even mention them anywhere in our review

The bottom line is, if something can be on your test, you'll find it in our modules; and if something is not going to be on your test, it's not going to be in our modules. Each and every math concept that even has the slightest possibility to be on the test can be found in our modules.

THE OFFICIAL REAL PRACTICE TESTS:
Although we don't suggest you refer to any other book, the only time we recommend using other books is for practicing previously administered tests to exercise your skills. The best resources for actual practice tests are the official guides published by the test makers that have several actual previously administered tests. One can *replicate* these tests as closely as one can, but no one other than the test administrators can *duplicate* them, and have the ability to reproduce or publish them. Therefore, to get the maximum effect of our approach, you must practice the actual tests from the official guide. You can also take a free online practice test by going to their website. EZ's practice tests are also based upon the most recently administered tests, and include every type of question that can be expected on the actual exam.

HOW OUR BOOKS CAN HELP YOU:
Our books are designed to help you identify your strengths and the areas which you need to work on. If you study all our modules, you will be fully equipped with all the tools needed to take your test head-on. Moreover, you'll also have the satisfaction that you did all you possibly could do to prepare yourself for the test, and you didn't leave any stone unturned. The amount of content covered in our books is far more than what you would learn by studying all the other test-prep books that are out there, put together, or by even taking an online or an actual prep course, and of course, spending thousands of dollars in the process. This will give you an idea of how material we have covered in our books.

STRUCTURE OF OUR MODULES:
All our modules are *structured in a highly organized and systematic manner*. The review is divided into different modules. Each module is divided into units. Each unit is further subdivided into chapters. Each chapter covers various topics, and in each specific topic, you are given all that you need to solve questions on that topic in detail – explaining key concepts, rules, and other EZ unique features. Also included in some topics are test-taking strategies specific to the topics discussed. Following each topic are solved sample examples with comprehensive explanations, which are exclusively based on that topic, and utilizing the concepts covered in that topic and section. Finally, there are practice exercises with thorough explanations containing real test-like questions for each topic and section, which are very similar to actual test questions. All units, chapters, and topics are chronologically numbered for easy reference.

Moreover, the modules, units, chapters, and topics are all arranged in sequence so that later modules, units, chapters, and topics assume familiarity with the material covered in earlier modules, units, chapters, and topics. Therefore, the best way to review is to work through from the beginning to the end.

SERIES > MODULES > UNITS > CHAPTERS > TOPICS > SUB-TOPICS > SOLVED EXAMPLES > PRACTICE EXERCISES

THE EZ DIFFERENCE:

DIFFERENCE BETWEEN EZ SOLUTIONS' PUBLICATIONS AND OTHER BOOKS:

Most of the other test-prep books suggest that your exam only tests your ability to take the test, and it does not test any actual content knowledge. In other words, they claim that your test is all about knowing the test-taking strategies, and it has very little to do with the actual knowledge of content; others claim that your test is all about knowing a few most commonly tested topics. While we have great respect for these books and the people who write or publish them, all these books have one thing in common: they all want to give their readers a quick shortcut to success. They actually want their readers to believe that just by learning a few strategies and memorizing some key formulas, they'll be able to ace their test. We are not sure if it's the fault of the people who write these books or the people who use them; but someone is definitely trying to fool someone – either those test-prep books for making the readers believe it, or the readers for actually believing it (no pun intended).

With a test as vast as this, it's simply not possible to cover the entire content in just a few pages. We all wish; however, in life, there really aren't any shortcuts to success, and your test is no exception to this rule. Nothing comes easy in life, and that is also precisely the case with your test. You have to do it the hard way by working your way through. Unfortunately, there is no magic potion, which we can give you to succeed in math! Therefore, if you want to do well on your test – be mentally, physically, and psychologically prepared to do some hard work. In this case, efforts and results are directly proportional, that is, greater the efforts you make, better your results are going to be.

While most test-preparation books present materials that stand very little resemblance to the actual tests, EZ's publication series present tests that accurately depict the official tests in both, degree of difficulty and types of questions.

Our EZ books are like no other books you have ever seen or even heard of. We have a completely different concept, and our books are structured using a totally different model. We have *re-defined the way test-prep books should be*.

STRATEGIES SEPARATED FROM CONTENT:

What we have done in our modules is, *separated the actual content-knowledge from the test-taking strategies*. We truly believe that a test-prep program should be more than just a *cheat-sheet of tricks, tips, and traps*. The test you are preparing for is not a simple game that you can master by learning these quick tactics. What you really need to do well on your test is a program that builds true understanding and knowledge of the content.

PERFECT EQUILIBRIUM BETWEEN STRATEGIES AND CONTENT:

In our modules, we've tried our best to present a *truly unique equilibrium* between two competing and challenging skills: test-taking strategies and comprehensive content-knowledge. We have *blended* the two most important ingredients that are essential for your success on your test. We have *enhanced* the old traditional approach to some of the most advanced forms of test-taking strategies. To top all this, we have *refined* our solved examples with detailed explanations to give you hands-on experience to real test-like questions before you take your actual test.

Other Books: Most of the other test-prep books primarily concentrate on teaching their readers how to *guess* and *use the process of elimination,* and they get so obsessed with the tactics that in the process they completely ignore the actual content. Majority of the content of these books consists of pages of guessing techniques.

EZ Books: With our EZ Content-Knowledge Modules, you'll find *100% pure content* that has a highly organized and structured approach to all the content areas, which actually teaches you the content you need to know to do well on your test. Therefore, if you are looking to learn more than just guessing by process of elimination, and if you are serious about developing your skills and confidence level for your exam, then our highly organized and structured test-prep modules is the solution. By studying our books, you'll learn a systematic approach to any question that you may see on your test, and acquire the tools that will help you get there.

EZ Solutions' publications are packed with important information, sophisticated strategies, useful tips, and extensive practice that the experts know will help you do your best on your test.

You should use whichever concept, fact, or tip from that section that you think is appropriate to answer the question correctly in the least possible time. If you've mastered the material in our review modules and strategy modules, you should be able to answer almost all (99.99%) of the questions.

LEARN BACKWARDS AND MOVE FORWARD: Smart students are the ones who make an honest attempt to learn what they read, and also learn from their mistakes, but at the same time, who moves ahead. Therefore, you should learn backwards, that is, learn from your past experiences, and move forward, that is, keep moving ahead without looking back!

ONE CONCEPT, EZ MULTIPLE METHODS:
Our books often give you a *choice of multiple methods* of answering the same question – you can pick the method that seems easiest to you. Our goal is not to *prescribe* any *hard-and-fast* method for taking the test, but instead, to give you the *flexibility and tools you can use to approach your test with confidence and optimism*.

STRATEGIES OR CONTENT?

In order to do well on your test, it is absolutely essential that you have a pretty good grasp of all the concepts laid out in our review modules. Our review modules contain everything you need to know, or must know to crack your test. They cover everything from basic arithmetic to logical reasoning, and everything in between. Nonetheless, that's not enough. You should be able to use these concepts in ways that may not be so familiar or well known to you. This is where our EZ Strategies kick in.

CONTENT VERSUS STRATEGIES:

There is a *succinct* difference between knowing the math content and knowing the math strategies.

Hypothetically speaking, let's assume there is a student named Alex, who learns only the test-taking strategies; and there is another student named Andria, who learns only the math-content. Now when the test time comes, Andria who learns only the math-content is extremely likely to do a lot better than Alex, who learns only the test-taking strategies.

The truth is that someone who has the knowledge of all the math content, but doesn't know anything about the strategies, will almost always do better on the test than someone who knows all the strategies but doesn't know the content properly.

Now let's assume there is another student named Alexandria, who learns both, the test-taking strategies and the math-content. Yes, now we are talking! This student, Alexandria, who knows both the strategies and the content, is guaranteed to do a lot better than Alex, who only knows the strategies, or Andria who only knows the content.

This brings us to our conclusion on this topic: don't just study the strategies, or just the content; you need to know both simultaneously – the strategies and the content, in order to do well on your test. How quickly and accurately you can answer the math questions will depend on your knowledge of the content and the strategies, and that will have an overall effect on your success on the test.

Hence, the equation to succeed on your test is: **Strategies + Content = Success!**

We are confident that if you study our books on test-taking strategies along with our books on content-knowledge, you'll have everything you possibly need to know in order to do well on your test, in fact, to ace your test, and come out with flying colors!

The good thing is that you made the smart decision to buy this book, or if you are reading this online, or in a bookstore, or in a library, you are going to buy one soon!

CONTENT-KNOWLEDGE REVIEW MODULES:

THOROUGH IN-DEPTH REVIEW:

Most other test-prep books briefly touch upon some of the concepts sporadically. On the other hand, our books start from the basics, but unlike other books, they do not end there – *we go deep inside, beyond just touching up the surface* – all the way from fundamental skills to some of the most advanced content that many other prep books choose to ignore. *Each concept is first explained in detail, and then analyzed for most effective understanding* – each and every concept is covered, and we haven't left any stone unturned. Overall, our program is more challenging – you simply get the *best-of-the-best*, and you get more of everything!

COMPREHENSIVE REVIEW:

Our Content-Knowledge Review Modules provide the *most comprehensive and complete review* of all the concepts, which you need to know to excel in your test. Each module is devoted to one of the main subject areas so that you can focus on the most relevant material. The ideal way to review our modules is to go through each topic thoroughly, understand all the solved examples, and work out all of the practice exercises. You must review each topic, understand every solved example, and work out all of the practice exercises. If you don't have enough time, just glimpse through a section. If you feel comfortable with it, move on to something else that may potentially give you more trouble. If you feel uncomfortable with it, review that topic more thoroughly.

Moreover, if you carefully work through our review, you will probably find some topics that you already know, but you may also find some topics that you need to review more closely. You should have a good sense of areas with which you are most comfortable, and in which areas you feel you have a deficiency. Work on any weaknesses you believe you have in those areas. This should help you organize your review more efficiently. Try to give yourself plenty of time and make sure to review the skills and master the concepts that you are required and expected to know to do well on your test. Of course, the more time you invest preparing for your test and more familiar you are with these fundamental principles, the better you will do on your test.

There is a lot of content reviewed in our modules. Although the amount of material presented in our books may appear to be overwhelming, it's the most complete review to get prepared for your test. To some of you, this may seem like a great deal of information to assimilate; however, when you start reviewing, you'll probably realize that you are already comfortable with many concepts discussed in our review modules. We also suggest that you spread your use of our modules over several weeks, and study different modules at your own pace. Even if you are sure you know the basic concepts, our review will help to warm you up so that you can go into your test with crisp and sharp skills. Hence, we strongly suggest that you at least touch up on each concept. However, depending on your strengths and weaknesses, you may be able to move quickly through some areas, and focus more on the others that seem to be troublesome to you. You should develop a plan of attack for your review of the wide range of content. Work on your weaknesses, and be ready to take advantage of your strengths.

Finally, our main objective in the content review modules is to refresh your knowledge of key concepts on the test and we attempt to keep things as concrete and concise as possible.

PRACTICE MODULES:

BASIC WORKBOOK:

Our math practice basic workbook contains a variety of questions on each and every topic that is covered in our review modules. The best way is to first learn all the concepts from our review modules and then apply your skills to test your knowledge on the actual test-like questions in our basic workbook.

ADVANCED WORKBOOK:

Our math practice advanced workbook also contains a variety of questions on each and every topic that is covered in our review modules. Once you become comfortable with the questions in our basic workbook, you should try your hands on our advanced workbook so that you can gain more experience with some of the most difficult questions. For students who are aiming for a very high score, practicing from our advanced workbook is very important. For students who are aiming for a mediocre score, practicing from our advanced workbook is not so important.

▪ABOUT THIS BOOK

In order to excel on your test, it's important that you master each component of your test. That's why we have broken the entire test into different sections and each book focuses only on only one component. It's important to learn the test content and the art of tackling the questions you'll see on the test; nevertheless, it's equally important to get a strong hold of the format and style of the test. Apparently it's not enough to only know the test content, you also need to have a solid knowledge of the test format, and know how to prepare for the test most efficiently. This book is exclusively dedicated to the **Test Format** that applies to the entire test.

WHAT'S COVERED IN THIS BOOK:

In this book, you will learn everything related to the **Test Format** that can be used on different types of questions throughout the test. Learning the content of this book will not only improve your performance on the test, but will also make you a smarter and wiser test-taker. In this book, you'll learn all the skills and strategies related to the test, so that you can tackle the question quickly, correctly, and more efficiently. In fact, being able to understand the nuts and bolts of the test is one of the most important factors to succeed on the test

WHAT'S NOT COVERED IN THIS BOOK:

This book does not cover any content, math or verbal – to learn about the content areas, you must refer to the other books in the series.

PRE-REQUISITES FOR THIS BOOK:

There is no pre-requisite for this book. In fact, this should be the first books that you should read once you start preparing for the test. Hence, when you go through this book, you are not expected to know anything about the test.

RELATED MODULES FOR THIS BOOK: You will get the best out of this book if you use it in conjunction with some of the other related books in the series that are listed below.

List of related modules for this book:
▪ EZ Solutions – Test Prep Series – Math Strategies
▪ EZ Solutions – Test Prep Series – Math Review – Arithmetic
▪ EZ Solutions – Test Prep Series – Math Review – Algebra
▪ EZ Solutions – Test Prep Series – Math Review – Applications
▪ EZ Solutions – Test Prep Series – Math Review – Geometry
▪ EZ Solutions – Test Prep Series – Math Review – Word Problems
▪ EZ Solutions – Test Prep Series – Math Review – Logic & Stats
▪ EZ Solutions – Test Prep Series – Math Practice – Basic Workbook
▪ EZ Solutions – Test Prep Series – Math Practice – Advanced Workbook

Note: Look at the back of the book for a complete list of EZ books

PART 0.0: INTRODUCTION TO TEST-TAKER'S MANUAL:

Please note that all the advices and suggestions given in this book are merely guidelines intended to give you general ideas about how to best approach the test, develop a good test preparation plan, and learn the test-taking strategies to prepare for the test in the most effective and efficient manner possible. Like most skills, test-taking skills also vary from person to person and from situation to situation. Some of the suggestions and strategies will work for you, while others may not. Feel free to select from among all the suggestions and strategies given in this book in order to have a plan that works best for you. A good approach would be to read each suggestion or strategy carefully, try it out, and see if it works well with you, and then make smart choices according to what works best for you.

No study guide can guarantee a perfect score, but we have done our best to provide you with the best test preparation material. We have developed a study guide system that goes beyond just the basic jargon, and goes a step ahead. Our books will teach you how to orchestrate all the individual test-taking skills, such as test information, test content, strategies, and other organizational skills into one collective and powerful way of approaching the test with the best knowledge and the right confidence. If you have our complete series of books, it will practically prepare you for everything that can be on the test, and you'll be able to demonstrate all your abilities and skills that you'll learn, not only from our books but also from your prior experiences over the years.

WHY LEARN TEST-TAKING SKILLS:

You may have learnt each and every concept that is given in your books. You may have memorized even the minutest detail that exists. There is no doubt that you have acquired all the content knowledge and you have worked very hard and learned a lot. But still, there's more to mastering a standardized test. There is one thing missing that may prevent you from getting a good score on standardized tests. There is one more thing that you need to do before you are ready to take your test, which is to study the test-taking skills given in this book. They will equip you with all the tools needed to do your best and get the score you really deserve. Learning test-taking skills will help you overcome the trickiness that often accompanies tests. Good test-taking skills will not guarantee that you will get a perfect score on every test, but they will ensure that you are able to perform at your best and that your test score most accurately reflects what you really know.

TEST-TAKING IS AN ART:

Test-taking in itself is an art, one which needs refinement. One cannot refine the art without proper review, practice, evaluation, and some very serious dedication. It's an art or skill that can be acquired and improved upon. Always remember, there are several techniques that you can apply before, during, and after the test to make sure that your test scores truly reflect your abilities and that will ultimately make you succeed in your career and profession. It's a game in which if you know the rules and abide by them, you can come out as a winner.

ACQUIRE THE TEST-TAKING SKILLS:

Even though the creators of your test claim to measure skills that you have developed over a long period of time, a short period of rigorous study from our books can make a remarkable difference in your final scores. Contrary to popular belief, these tests do not measure innate skills; instead, they mostly measure acquired skills. No one comes with this in-born talent, not even expert test-takers. If someone is good at standardized tests, it's simply because they've already acquired these skills from somewhere, knowingly or unknowingly, maybe from a class, or by doing a lot of research, or simply making use of the best and the easiest way – by using EZ Solutions books. If you happen to be one of those people who are struggling with standardized tests, you have nothing to worry about; you just have to make the right kind of effort to acquire them now. Test-taking skills are not rocket science – anyone can acquire them with some time and effort. One should try to acquire and develop these skills as early as possible since they are skills that can be developed, but it would still need some time. Learning our test-taking skills can make you less stressful and more successful.

TEST-TAKING SKILLS ARE REQUIRED THROUGHOUT YOUR LIFETIME:

Historically, test-taking is considered to be a skill that will help you throughout your life, from taking a written driver's test to taking a standardized test to getting into college to a complicated job placement test. Without this skill or ability, one can be severely handicapped.

TEST CONTENT KNOWLEDGE IS ESSENTIAL:

Doing well on standardized tests does not necessarily depend only on how much you know. In order to do well, you need to know not only the material very well, but also how to apply your knowledge to work in a smart and efficient way. Learning these test-taking skills will make you more knowledgeable, and a smarter test-taker. This book will bring out the most in yourself so that you can perform at your best.

TEST-WISENESS:

Test-wiseness is the ability to use the characteristics and format of a cognitive test to maximize one's score. It's a fact that some students are better than others at taking tests. Students clearly vary in test-wiseness, and such variations are reflected in performance on tests. Test-wiseness is not a substitute for knowledge of the subject matter. However, test-taking skills will definitely make you test-wiser.

WHEN TO APPLY TEST-TAKING STRATEGIES:

While you do need to know the content included on the test in order to do well, knowing some proven test-taking strategies can help you get a better score. Whenever you know how to answer a question directly, just answer it. The test-taking strategies that are reviewed in this book should be used only when you need them. Different kinds of tests require different kinds of test-taking strategies. Also, merely knowing the test-taking strategies is not enough, you must also know "how" and "when" to apply them for the most effective results.

LEARN NEW TECHNIQUES FOR TEST-TAKING AND STUDYING:

Learn new ways to prepare yourself for tests if the old ways are not working adequately. If you study the same old way, you will probably get the same results. New techniques can save you time as well as improve your performance. Hence, change your approach and try some of the suggestions given in our books for varied results.

STUDY SKILLS, TEST-TAKING SKILLS, AND ORGANIZATIONAL SKILLS ARE INTERDEPENDENT:

Study skills, test-taking skills, and organizational skills are interdependent. You need to acquire all three skills at the same time, not just one without the others, as one skill cannot be substituted by another. Don't expect that one or two strong areas will take care of, or balance out, the weak areas. If you are weak in one area, then work on that first. Prepare thoroughly for your tests; there is no alternative to studying. For instance, if you get a geometry question that requires you to know the Pythagorean Theorem, you may have learned all your test-taking strategies but if you don't even know the theorem, there is very little you can do to solve that question. Therefore, knowing your test content is absolutely essential.

PART 1.0: GENERAL INFORMATION ABOUT THE TEST:

TABLE OF CONTENTS:

THIS PAGE HAS BEEN INTENTIONALLY LEFT BLANK.

1.1: TEST OVERVIEW:

The following is general test information. It should answer most of your questions about the test. We made every effort to provide you with the most accurate and up-to-date information in a very clear and precise manner.

While every effort has been made to ensure that the contents of this book are as up-to-date as possible, we hold no responsibility for any inaccuracies in the information given below. We strongly urge you to check with the official test administrator for more accurate/current information about the test.

TEST FORMAT:

Most graduate level standardized tests (such as GMAT and GRE) are no longer given in paper-and-pencil format (except in a few countries outside the United States). Instead, a new Computer-Adaptive Test format, also known as CAT is now used. Most undergraduate standardized tests (such as SAT and ACT) are usually given in both formats, in paper-and-pencil format (except in a few countries outside the United States) as well as in computer-based format.

Your test is a standardized assessment test that helps colleges/universities assess the qualifications of applicants for advanced studies. Colleges/universities use this test as one of the measures of predicting academic performance in their undergraduate/graduate programs.

TEST DEVELOPMENT PROCESS:

Your test is developed by experts who use standardized procedures to guarantee high quality, widely suitable test material. All questions are subjected to independent reviews and are revised or discarded as needed. Multiple choice questions are tested during actual test administrations. The Writing task topics are tried out on first year students and then assessed for their fairness and reliability.

Each multiple-choice question used in the standardized tests is thoroughly reviewed by professional test developers. It is also one of the most rigorously researched and analyzed standardized tests in the world. Each question on the test goes through an in-depth pre-testing and review process to ensure that every single question is fair to all students across genders and ethnicity groups. New multiple choice questions are tested each time the test is administered. Answers to experimental questions are not counted in the scoring of your test, but the experimental questions are not identified and could appear anywhere in the test.

WHAT YOUR TEST MEASURES:

Your test is designed to measure the skills that may help students succeed in a challenging curriculum. It assesses skills developed over time, and it's a valid and reliable predictor of success in undergraduate/graduate programs.

Your test is designed to measure the basic quantitative, verbal, and analytical writing skills that one develops or acquires in the course of your academic career both in and out of school, at work, or otherwise over a long period of time, without emphasizing memorized data. It measures knowledge of subjects learned in the classroom/work, including reading, writing, and math, and how well you can apply that knowledge outside of the classroom. It is an effective way of providing admission officers with an objective measure of academic abilities to supplement subjective criteria used in the selection process, such as interviews, grades, and references. It also helps colleges get to know you better by giving them insight into how you think, solve problems, and communicate.

The purpose of your test is to measure the basic mathematical, verbal, and analytical writing skills that one develops over a long period of time in school and work and your ability to think systematically and to employ these skills that you have acquired throughout your years of schooling.

It should be noted that the test does not aim to measure any specialized skills such as interpersonal skills, job skills, business skills, etc., or your knowledge of specific business or academic subjects. It does not measure any specific content in undergraduate or graduate course work or subjective qualities such as motivation, creativity, and interpersonal skills. Neither specific business experience is necessary, nor will any specific academic subject area be covered. However, you are assumed to know basic mathematics (arithmetic, algebra, and geometry) with no advanced mathematical skills (such as calculus), to know the basic conventions of standard written English, and to be able to write an analytical essay.

WHO IS REQUIRED TO TAKE THIS TEST:

Test scores are used by admissions officers in thousands of colleges/universities for thousands of graduate/undergraduate programs worldwide. Nowadays, most colleges and universities use the test scores as a criterion of admission into their programs. It is required by colleges and universities to measure the academic achievement and proficiency of individuals entering or completing graduate/undergraduate programs.

Any accredited college or university, or any department or division within a college or university, may require or recommend that its applicants take this test. The scores can be used by admissions or fellowship panels to supplement undergraduate records and other qualifications for graduate study. The scores provide common measures for comparing the qualifications of applicants and aid in the evaluation of grades and recommendations.

WHY COLLEGES REQUIRE STANDARDIZED TEST SCORES:

Standardized test helps in evaluating which candidates are most likely to succeed academically in respective programs. Schools that require applicants to submit test scores in the application process are generally interested in admitting the most competitive and best-qualified applicants into their programs. Standardized test have proven to be a reliable measurement to assess candidates' abilities and predict their success in college. For most colleges, standardized test is recognized as the single most effective test available for matching student abilities with program contents – regardless of the candidate's educational background, race, gender, cultural or national origin. For you, as a student, this means you may find a more beneficial and competitive learning environment at schools that require standardized test scores as part of your application process. Thus, the requirements of standardized test scores prove to be advantageous for both, the schools and the students.

WHAT STANDARD TEST SCORES INDICATE:

Since standardized test gauges skills that are important to a successful study of different programs at the graduate/undergraduate level, the standardized test scores will give a good indication of how well-prepared you are to succeed academically. The standardized test scores, along with your prior grades, is the best predictor of success in a college. The standardized test gives you an opportunity to show colleges what you know and what you know you can do. Keep in mind that taking the standardized test is the first step in finding the program – the one where you'll best succeed and discover the tools necessary to pursue your passions and achieve your career goals.

IMPORTANCE OF STANDARDIZED TEST SCORES:

Standardized test scores vary in importance for different programs at different schools in different countries. Although many factors play a role in the admissions decisions, the standardized test score is usually an important one, most of the good schools rely heavily on standardized test scores, and consider them as one of the most important admission criteria. In addition to good standardized test scores, schools normally also consider other factors, such as work experience, prior GPA score, letters of recommendation, essay, interviews, etc. Standardized test scores are also considered to be a major factor in determining the eligibility for financial aid. The kind of standardized test scores you need to get depends on the type of college/university you want to get into. Contact the specific school for more accurate admission requirements.

Correlation Between Standardized Test Scores and Academic Success: According to some studies, higher standardized test scores strongly correlate with the probability of success in graduate business school: the higher you score, the more likely you are to complete your program/degree successfully, and vice versa. For this reason alone, many colleges/universities require applicants to take standardized test.

1.2: PARTS OF STANDARDIZED TESTS:

Standardized tests are usually divided into the following three sections:

(A) QUANTITATIVE SECTION:

The types of questions that appear in the quantitative section of the test are designed to test your reasoning ability.

Test Measures: The Quantitative section measures your:
- understanding of mathematical skills.
- ability to think analytically and reason quantitatively.
- ability to solve problems in a quantitative setting.
- ability to use and reason with numbers or mathematical concepts.
- ability to read, understand, and solve a problem that involves either an actual or an abstract situation.
- ability to interpret graphic data.

Topics Tested: The Quantitative questions require a basic knowledge of the principles and fundamentals of arithmetic, algebra, geometry, and data interpretation. You do not need to know any advanced mathematics.

(B) VERBAL SECTION:

Test Measures: The Verbal section measures your:
- ability to read and comprehend written material.
- ability to reason and evaluate arguments.
- ability to use words as tools in reasoning.
- ability to read quickly and efficiently.
- ability to analyze and evaluate written material and synthesize information obtained from it.
- ability to recognize and analyze relationships among different parts of sentences and paragraphs.
- ability to understand scholarly prose and to work with specialized and technical vocabulary.
- ability to correct written material to conform to standard written English.

Topics Tested: The Verbal questions require a basic knowledge of the principles and fundamentals of reading, grammar, and vocabulary.

(C) WRITING SECTION:

Test Measures: The Writing section measures your:
- ability to think critically and to communicate complex ideas.
- ability to understand and analyze issues and arguments.
- ability to understand, draw, and infer logical conclusions.
- ability to make rational assessments about unfamiliar, fictitious relationships and to logically present your perspective.
- ability to composition of an issue.
- ability to take a position on the basis of the details of the issue, and present a critique of the conclusion derived from a specific way of thinking.

Note: Always remember that the test administrators sometimes change the content, administrative procedure, and other details about the test too quickly for any published book to keep up with. Although every effort is made to keep the information in this book up-to-date; however, changes may occur after the book is published. For the latest, up-to-date information about the test you are taking, visit EZ Solution's website at www.EZmethods.com.

THIS PAGE HAS BEEN INTENTIONALLY LEFT BLANK.

PART 2.0: HOW TO PREPARE FOR THE TEST:

TABLE OF CONTENTS:

THIS PAGE HAS BEEN INTENTIONALLY LEFT BLANK.

2.1: GET INVOLVED IN YOUR TEST STUDY:

You should study hard, stay disciplined, and take your test seriously – so that you can excel in your test, and be successful in your career! In order to be well prepared for the test, you must get meticulously involved in the test preparation, and give the test your absolute best, and your complete heart and soul. It's well worth to try to do your best on a test that can have such a great impact on both your academic and professional career. There is no mystery or secret to doing well on the test. Some hard work can make luck unnecessary. Luck is not a substitute but a complement to hard work. We have outlined several different aspects of successful test preparation throughout this book.

STUDY HOW:
Different students comprehend differently using different methods, whichever methods help them understand and retain the material most effectively.
(A) **Audio Method:** Some students comprehend the material better if they talk and recite aloud.
(B) **Visual Method:** Some students comprehend better if they read or write what they study; for such students, the best alternative is to read the EZ series of books extensively.
(C) **Interactive Method:** Some students comprehend the material better if they hear it from another person in an easy to understand manner; for such students, the best alternative is to join a study group or get some private tutoring from us.

STUDY FROM:
We highly recommend that you study from our set of self-study test-prep material, since it's the most complete and comprehensive test-prep material ever developed. However, you can also use any other supplementary test-prep material and review other references and sources, especially the study guides written by the test makers.

EZ STUDY PROGRAM:
The EZ Solutions test-prep books can be used in several different ways, based on your schedule, time constraints, and strengths/weaknesses. Consider these books as small units of a very big test.

ONE BOOK PER WEEK PROGRAM:
Ideally, you should neither study too much material in too little time, which will result in cramming and confusion, nor should you study too little material in too much time, which will result in forgetting the material you learned when you first started. The best fit would be to follow a moderate pace by studying enough material in enough time. The word, "enough," here is relative – every individual has a different pace of working and comprehending. In general, perhaps the best way to study using EZ Solutions series of books is by studying one book per week by spending two and a half hours every day. This will give you ample time to study, comprehend, and review each and every part of the book, and practice all questions and go through answer explanations. Make sure to follow the strategic order which we have specified at the beginning of each book and review each book completely before moving on to another book. Each subsequent book assumes knowledge of all previous modules.

(A) **Accelerated Program:** If you are a fast worker or if you don't have enough time between now and your test date, you can easily accelerate your speed by studying one book every three to four days, by spending three to four hours every day.

(B) **Decelerated Program:** If you are a somewhat slow worker or if you have plenty of time between now and your test date, you can easily decelerate your speed by studying one book every two weeks, by spending about one hour every day.

STUDY ACTIVELY NOT PASSIVELY:
You should study actively and not passively. It is very easy to enter the passive mode without even realizing it, where your eyes can roll over the words you read, while you think that the answer will somehow pop up in your brain automatically without making much effort. If you have a tendency to subconsciously fall into the passive mode, you should try to fight it by trying to be conscientious and alert. It is very important for you to be actively reading, especially while reading a question on the test.

DO NOT PROCRASTINATE:

It's fairly easy to put off your test preparation and do something more interesting such as watching movies or television, shopping, partying, spending time with friends, etc. Surprisingly enough, even cleaning your room or organizing your closet may seem more interesting than studying for the test. Before you realize, the days will pass quickly, and soon you'll see the test day approaching, and one fine day you'll find yourself overwhelmed by just how much material you have to cover and hysterically start cramming just a few days before the test. If you are particularly addicted to procrastination and not studying, it may be a good idea that you arrange to study with a friend. It also may be beneficial to join or organize a study group and play an active role in managing the affair. This will not only make you accountable to a group of people but it will also make you feel more competitive.

2.2: STUDY ENVIRONMENT:

PROPER STUDY ENVIRONMENT:
Everyone needs a different study environment that works best for them, and it is very important that you find the one that works best for you.

STUDY-PLACE:
The immediate environment in which you study can have a big impact on how efficiently you study. Study at a place where you can concentrate, get interested in the material, and give it your complete attention.

Make your study setting conducive to studying and check to make sure your study-place meets the following conditions:

(A) **Comfort:** Your study-place should be equipped with a comfortable desk and a chair. It should also have plenty of room so that you are not cramped or uncomfortable.

(B) **Temperature:** Your study-place should have a comfortable room temperature, not too cold and not too warm, just right.

(C) **Lighting:** Your study-place should be well-lit for you to see everything clearly and stay alert, so that you don't get strained or drowsy.

(D) **Noise:** Your study-place should have absolute silence, free of any noises coming from the television, radio, phone, etc.

(E) **Interruptions:** Your study-place should be as far away from any potential auditory or visual distractions or disturbances as possible – switch off your cell phones, switch on your answering machine, and ask your roommates or friends/family not to disturb you while you are studying.

(F) **Disturbance:** Consider a "do not disturb" sign outside your door.

(G) **Neatness:** Your study-place should be neat and clean so that you feel organized and are able to concentrate on your studies.

STUDY EQUIPMENT:
Keep all your study material at your study place so that you have a proper study environment and you don't spend your time going in and out getting things. Have everything that you need available at your study-place, such as, books, pencils, pens, paper, dictionary, calculator, voice recorder, coffee etc.

Last but not the least – don't get so comfortable that you fall asleep!

2.3: STUDY TIME & CRAMMING:

HOW MUCH TIME TO SPEND ON PREPARING FOR THE TEST:
- How much time you should spend in preparing for the test would depend on where you stand and how fast you can learn. Hence, it would be hard to say how much time one should spend in preparing for the test as it would be different for each individual.
- On an average, it is recommended that one should spend 2½ hours each day for at least 8 weeks. Of course, you can study more hours each day and be prepared for the test sooner.
- Remember, the more time you spend studying for the test, the more prepared and relaxed you will feel on the day of the test, and the better you will be able to perform on the test; hence, better your chances of getting a good score.

SPLIT THE TEST:
You have a huge test and have an overwhelming job to take care of. The best way to manage this big task is by breaking it into smaller units. Practically as well as mentally, it's easier to manage smaller units of a big task instead of taking it head-on. In fact, this is the basic foundation upon which EZ Solutions books have been formulated. We have divided your entire test in smaller and more manageable modules. So, if you are making use of our set of books, you'll automatically be following this rule.

CHOOSE A GOOD TIME TO STUDY:
- Set aside a few hours to study every morning, afternoon, evening, or night – whatever time works best for you.
- Be aware of your best time of the day to study when you are most attentive and productive.
- Choose a time to study when your concentration and productivity level is at its peak – for some individuals, this may be early morning, while for others it could be afternoon, evening, or late night.
- Develop a routine that works best for you, stick to it, be consistent, and use your time wisely.

DESIGN A REALISTIC STUDY SCHEDULE:
- Design and plan a realistic schedule giving top priority to your study time. Plan an hourly schedule of activities for each day of your test preparation time. Systematically list each activity such as, study, employment, recreation, socialization, sports, and personal time.
- Be realistic while making your schedule.
- Have a study schedule that makes use of "wasted time".
- Try to make your schedule flexible enough to allow for any last-minute changes, such as surprise birthday parties or some unexpected work. You should be prepared to postpone some non-academic activities which can wait until you are done with your test.
- Create a test-prep calendar to plan your entire test-prep and to ensure that you're ready to take the test at least a week before the test day.
- On an actual calendar, mark the days you are going to prepare for the test.
- It would be a good idea to include a few days off.
- Stick to your schedule; like with any other project, little is gained if it isn't organized or methodical.
- Based on how much preparation you need and based on your strengths and weaknesses, establish a detailed study plan and select appropriate material for each session.
- Re-evaluate your progress from time to time and revise your study plan accordingly.

BALANCE YOUR TIME:
- Preparing for standardized tests may require more time than any other regular test, but it doesn't mean that every single remaining minute should be devoted only to studying.
- We suggest that you devote more time to studying; however, don't completely deprive yourself of everything else.

PRIORITIZE YOUR TIME:
- Prioritize your time based upon how much you need to study and how crucial it is for you to get your desired score.
- Prioritize your study time based on your strengths and weaknesses, and determine what areas need more time.

QUALITY AND NOT QUANTITY OF STUDY TIME IS MORE IMPORTANT:

- While studying for your test, the quality and not the quantity of time you spend studying is more important. You can study for 10 hours straight but your productivity may only be worth 2 hours. Therefore, whatever time you decide to spend on studying, make sure the productivity rate is pretty high.
- For any normal individual, it's impossible to study 24 hours a day, but it should not be hard to devote 6-8 hours if you plan your time efficiently.

AVOID CRAMMING AND FOLLOW A MODERATE PACE:

- Spread your study sessions over an extended period – days, weeks, or even months.
- Review for several short periods rather than a few long periods. Don't practice extremely mini or marathon study sessions. Avoid cramming, try to break up and spread your study sessions into several short manageable time segments and meaningful units rather than a few long and tiring time segments.
- By following a moderate pace, you will not only save yourself the agony of having to cram everything at the last moment, you will also be able to retain more information and get less fatigued.
- Cramming leads to temporary knowledge which fades away; long term studying leads to long term knowledge and understanding about the subject that will probably stay with you for a long period of time or even for the rest of your life.

STUDY TIME LENGTH:

- Don't overwhelm yourself with too much information in too little time.
- It is recommended that you should not study for less than half an hour or more than two hours at a stretch.
- It is hard to do something meaningful in less than a half an hour study session. By the time you warm up and actually start learning something, you'll realize it's time to go.
- Based on research, an average individual's productivity level drops after continuous study for two hours at a stretch, after which they need a break.
- Real learning occurs through studying that takes place over a period of time rather than all at one time.
- Keep a moderate and steady pace rather than a crash pace. Rushing, either while studying or while taking a test, will work against you.
- Studying while you are mentally fatigued is usually a waste of time. You should instead take a break and study once you feel refreshed.

TAKE BREAKS:

- Arrange for strategic breaks during 1 to 2 hour study periods.
- If you study for more than an hour or two, give yourself a break for a few minutes before continuing. During your break time, try to relax, take a walk, and perhaps have a snack.

DISADVANTAGES OF CRAMMING:

- Cramming only helps in short term memory, it does not help in learning, understanding, or retaining information over a long period of time.
- Cramming also often leads to confusion, increased levels of stress, and it interferes with clear thinking.
- Cramming new material may interfere with you recalling the material you have already learned properly.
- Cramming everything the night before the test can also blank you out while taking the test.
- Cramming won't help you much except to make you so tired that when you take the test you won't be able to think clearly enough to answer the questions you actually know.
- Your test is very detailed and comprehensive and it can't be mastered by "cramming" in the last few minutes/days.

2.4: TEST GOALS:

PUT YOUR GOALS IN WRITING:
Putting goals in writing will increase your commitment towards achieving them. It will also act as a constant reminder of the goals that you have set for yourself and will minimize the chances of losing sight of your goals in the shuffle of daily activities.

GOALS SHOULD BE CHALLENGING BUT REALISTICALLY ACHIEVABLE:
Make your goals challenging but at the same time make sure they are realistically achievable and attainable. They should neither be too easy, nor too difficult to achieve. Your goals should make you work harder in order to achieve them. A challenging and attainable goal will also hold your interest and keep you motivated. Make sure that your goals have a close correlation with one of the most important measures, which is, your own capabilities.

INDUCE REALISTIC GOALS NOT UNREALISTIC DEMANDS:
It would be unrealistic to say: "I must get 100% in math" – especially when you know that you have never achieved higher than 70% in math. Clearly, you are making unrealistic demands on yourself. Unrealistic demands made by others can also lead to unrealistic self-statements. The above unrealistic statement could be changed to: "I'll do my best to get at least 5% more than last time in each practice test I take." Now you are making a realistically achievable demand on yourself, by setting small leaps. Remember, Rome wasn't built in one day; it will take time to go from 70% to 95%, but you can do it.

GOALS SHOULD BE CLEAR AND SPECIFIC:
(A) **Clear Goals:** Your goals should be very clear, and not ambiguous. If your goals are clear, you will have a better idea of what you need to do in order to achieve them.
(B) **Specific Goals:** Your goals should be as specific as possible, and not too broad and general. For instance, don't make a goal which says that you want to do well on your test – this goal is too broad. Instead, get more specific and make a goal that specifies:
  - What kind of score you want on the test, how much on math and how much on verbal.
  - Skills you need to acquire.
  - Target date by when you should be able to achieve it.
  - What you want to accomplish in the remaining time.

GOALS SHOULD HAVE A TARGET DATE AND DEADLINE:
Your goals must have a target date and a deadline by which you should achieve them. A goal is not really a goal in real terms until you set a deadline and a target date for its accomplishment. If it goes on indefinitely and does not have a deadline, it's not really a goal. So make sure you fix a target date and a deadline by which you must meet your goals.

GOALS SHOULD BE MEASURE-ABLE & TRACK-ABLE:
(A) **Measure-able:** Your goals should be measurable, and you must check frequently if you are able to achieve your goals. If you feel you are lagging behind compared to what you had set previously, you need to work harder.
(B) **Track-able:** Make sure to track your progress in your calendar and find a way to reward yourself as you finish the tasks.

GOALS SHOULD BE FLEXIBLE:
You should revise, update, and modify your goals as and when needed. Once you set your initial goals and as you progress through your test preparation program, you will have a better idea about your test content, and over time, you may then realize that the goals you had set for yourself previously were too high or too low based on what you are actually capable of. In either case, your goals are not written in stone – from time to time feel free to modify, revise, or update your goals so that they are more in tune with what you think you can realistically achieve.

GOALS SHOULD BE SELF-SET NOT IMPOSED:
It is very important that your goals are set by you and they are not imposed by anyone else, and that your goals are not based on any other criteria. You are in the best position to decide what may represent your objectives and then work towards achieving them. Self-set goals are more achievable, attainable, and realistic. If others have set expectations for you that are counter-productive, you may need to talk with them and come to a new agreement about how to define

your success. It doesn't matter if you'll be able to meet other people's expectations, what's more important is that you've met your own expectations and that you do your absolute best, and get a score that you think you deserve.

GOALS SHOULD ACT AS A MOTIVATOR:

Your goals should act as a motivating factor. Set your goals so that they motivate you and become a challenge that you must meet. You'll feel more confident when you know you're actively preparing for the test and increasing your performance to earn a higher score.

GOALS SHOULD BE COMPATIBLE:

Check your other major goals for compatibility. Don't fall into the trap of setting major goals where the achievement of one will prevent the attainment of another.

REWARD YOURSELF:

- Set up a reward system for dedicated studying and meeting your deadlines – for instance think of a reward that you would give yourself after finishing each chapter or section – watch a movie, go out to eat, or visit a friend.
- Set up a reward system for good test performance – for instance think of a reward that you would give yourself if you achieve a particular score on your next practice test or actual test – treat yourself, buy a new electronic gadget, or take a much deserved vacation.
- Last, but not the least, after you get a good score, life will automatically reward you with bright future prospects – such as, better school or college, more scholarship and financial aids, better jobs and promotions, etc.

2.5: OTHER ELEMENTS OF TEST-PREP:

Test preparation is not all about studying and learning the test material. It goes far beyond just that. Test preparation also often involves other elements such as physical, emotional, mental, social, and financial preparedness – not just the night before the test, but all throughout your test preparation period. For instance, the amount of sleep and exercise you get or what you eat – not just the day before the test, but for days and even weeks or months before the test, will make a big difference in how you feel – and that's what will give you the power you need to perform well on the test day.

You may not realize it but these other elements are just as important as studying for your test. Students preparing for a test often neglect these aspects. To do your best, you must attend to these aspects and not take them lightly. Don't forget the basics and think of yourself as a total person – not just a test-taker. You should do whatever it takes to get a good score.

Studying for a test is analogous and comparable to playing a tennis match, performing on a stage, participating in a debate, or playing a game of chess. The best way to ace any of these activities is by preparing and planning actively: keeping a fit body, having a nutritious diet, taking ample rest, exercising your mind, gaining confidence, learning how to deal with stress, learning the required skills, applying the right strategies, and practicing the skills until you become perfect. Guess what? The same rules pretty much apply to preparing for a big and important test, just like the one you are preparing for.

The following components are important in order to prepare you for the test in all aspects and all forms, from head to toe.

(A) PHYSICAL PREPAREDNESS:
Yes, taking a test is not like playing a game of soccer; nevertheless, physical preparation is one of the main components of an effective test preparation program. Consider your body as the support system of your mind. If your body is in good condition, so will your mind. Physical preparation will keep your mind and body in sync and also help in reducing test anxiety. Physical preparation is not something that can be attained overnight – it needs to be incorporated over a period of time. People who keep themselves in good physical condition often enjoy a competitive edge over their competitors. Everyone does better when they are in good shape, and test-taking is no exception. It's difficult for your mind to function properly when your body is not nurtured adequately. Remember, physical fitness is the stepping stone to mental fitness.

Physical preparation involves the following:

(i) Regular Exercise: You must do regular exercise.
- Exercise is great for reducing your stress, building your energy, and sharpening your mind.
- Exercise will stimulate your mind and body, boost your energy level, and improve your ability to think and concentrate.
- Plan time to exercise regularly and stay in good physical condition.
- Try workouts, weightlifting, aerobics, yoga, hiking, running, jogging, biking, soccer, tennis, etc.

(ii) Healthy Diet: You must have a healthy diet.
- Follow a healthy and nutritious diet which is rich in proteins and other essential vitamins.
- Foods rich in carbohydrates will also give extra energy that you may need to deal with your study session.

(iii) Regular and Sufficient Rest: You must take regular and sufficient rest.
- Get adequate amount of rest and enough sleep all throughout your test preparation time, this will help you remain alert and feel fresh.

EXERCISE YOUR MIND:
Exercise your mind to keep it in active mode by reading, problem solving, cracking logical puzzles, group discussions, etc.

BUILD UP YOUR CONCENTRATION AND STAMINA LEVEL:
(i) Concentration Level: Most of the standardized tests are at least 2-4 hours long or even longer if you include the administrative time. If you have a problem concentrating for long time periods, you should get accustomed to it and be able to build up your concentration level for these extended periods of time. Be sharp and focused throughout your test time; you should be just as sharp and focused at the end of your test as you were at the beginning. The ability to be attentive during the entire test is one of the keys to your success on the test. If you know the content

really well but are not able to concentrate on the test, you won't be able to perform at your optimum level and get the score you truly deserve.

(ii) Stamina Level: It's important that you work towards building up your test-taking stamina. Overall, the test can be a rather exhausting experience, and it's easy for some test-takers to run out of energy when they approach the latter part of the test. To avoid this from happening to you, you must work on building your test-taking stamina by doing several things. Apart from the physical preparedness that you read in the previous paragraph, you must also take as many full-length practice tests as possible, especially a week or more before your test date. This will make your mind and body get accustomed to working long hours on the actual test without losing energy midway.

NOTE FOR SMOKERS:

- Individuals who are smokers must remember that smoking will be strictly prohibited during the entire test. If you do decide to go during the test time to smoke, you will be losing on some very valuable time which you must invest in answering the questions and not further damaging your lungs. Those few minutes when you do decide to go out for a smoke can be very crucial to your test scores. In fact, every second on the test time is very critical, and can significantly affect your test scores. This means that you will not be allowed to smoke for the entire 2-4 hour test period, depending on the type of test you are taking.
- It would be a good idea to practice giving up smoking for 4-5 hours at a stretch and getting used to it so that it doesn't make your anxiety or frustration level soar due to not being able to smoke while taking your test. In fact, this may be a good opportunity to quit smoking altogether!

(B) EMOTIONAL PREPAREDNESS:

- Emotional preparation has a lot to do with your stress and anxiety level. You must be in an emotionally healthy state of mind in order to be truly prepared for the test. Test anxiety is a perfect example of the ways in which our thoughts can influence our feelings and our reactions to events.
- If you experience excessive anxiety, you should first try to go through our test anxiety section and then try to work on it as much as you can in order to control your emotions and not let it effect your preparation or performance on the test.

(C) MENTAL PREPAREDNESS:

- Test preparation also includes mental preparation. You should prepare your mind for the test so that you can make an effective study plan and better prepare yourself for the test on time.

(D) SOCIAL PREPAREDNESS:

- Since preparing for a test involves a lot of time and effort, you may have to prepare yourself socially as well. You should be able to strike a healthy balance between work, study, family, friends, entertainment, and other social events.
- You have a big and important task in front of you, which must be executed effectively. You have a choice to make in life, between your future career and your social life. You can either dedicate all your time and energy towards your test for a couple of months and then party all you want, or keep partying and have the same life or even worse in the days to come. It is your choice to make, but we would suggest you go with the former and not the latter.
- Try to postpone some activities if they interfere too much in your studies. Moreover, if you give yourself enough time to prepare yourself for the test on a regular basis, you may not even have to significantly change your social life.

(E) FINANCIAL/ECONOMICAL PREPAREDNESS:

- There is also some level of financial preparation involved. You should be prepared to invest some money towards your test preparation.
- The basic requirements would be to buy some relevant books and pay the test registration fee. Some people may also need external help in the form of a prep course or private tutoring, which can sometime turn into a costly affair.
- The most cost effective way to prepare for the test would be to buy EZ Solutions set of books as they are far less expensive and far more comprehensive than any prep course or private tutoring.
- You may also need to take some time off from work and there could be a cost involved in that as well. But at the end when you get a good score, all of this would be worth your while. Think of it as an investment towards your career or profession.
- It is a better deal to invest some money into your career now, and enjoy a better life in the years to come.

2.6: MOST COMMON TEST-TAKING ERRORS:

The following are the most common test-taking errors that the majority of test-takers make and they lose some very valuable points. Recognizing these errors in advance will prevent you from making them. You can perhaps learn to catch these errors yourself once you get enough exposure and experience with standardized tests; however, learning about them ahead of time will save you a lot of time by not committing them yourself. These errors constitute about 99% of the sum of all errors made on standardized tests.

#1: CONCEPT ERRORS:

Concept errors are made when you do not know or understand the appropriate concepts, properties, characteristics, rules, or principles required to answer the questions correctly. These types of mistakes occur when you do not spend enough time studying and reviewing the test material.
To Avoid Concept Errors: You must completely learn each and every concept pertaining to the test by thoroughly going through our review books.

#2: APPLICATION ERRORS:

Application errors are made when you do know the concepts required but you do not know or understand how to apply the concepts to answer the questions correctly.
To Avoid Application Errors: After completely learning each concept clearly, you must learn how, when, where, and which one to apply in actual questions by getting enough practice from our workbooks.

#3: TEST-TAKING STRATEGY ERRORS:

Test-taking strategy errors are made when you do know how to answer the question correctly but somehow you choose the incorrect answer because either you do not have enough information about using the appropriate test-taking strategies or you deviate from the proven test-taking strategies that you have already learned.
To Avoid Test-Taking Strategy Errors: You must learn all the test-taking strategies given in our strategy books. Also don't try out new techniques during the test – use tried and tested techniques that have worked well for you in the past.

#4: CARELESS ERRORS:

Careless errors are made when you do know how to answer the question correctly but you make some silly mistakes because you were not careful enough.
To Avoid Careless Errors: Answer the questions carefully and always try to review them in order to catch careless errors, if any. Careless errors can be very easily and automatically caught upon reviewing the test carefully. Be careful, and don't be careless.

#5: MECHANICAL ERRORS:

Mechanical errors are made when you successfully get the correct answer but fail to record your answer correctly on the answer sheet or on the computer screen.
To Avoid Mechanical Errors: After getting your answer, be very careful while transferring your answer from your scratch paper or the test booklet to the appropriate spot on the answer sheet by marking the corresponding oval on the answer sheet clearly, neatly, and completely, or on the computer screen by clicking on the correct answer choice. If you skip a question, make sure to skip the corresponding oval on the answer sheet.

#6: MISREAD QUESTION ERRORS:

Misread question errors are made when you partly read, misread, or misunderstand the question, and somehow answer the question with something other than what is asked.
To Avoid Misread Question Errors: Read and understand the question carefully and completely before trying to answer it.

#7: CHANGING ANSWER ERRORS:

Changing answer errors are made while changing your test answers from the correct to the incorrect ones. Sometimes you try to second guess a question that you had previously answered, and due to last minute confusion, you end up changing the answer from the correct to the incorrect one.
To Avoid Changing Answer Errors: Change answers only if you can prove to yourself that the changed answer is correct and you had actually made a mistake the first time you chose your answer. Never second guess your answer – your first guess is normally correct. For more information, refer to "changing answers" section later in this book.

2.7: MOST COMMON LACK OF TEST-TAKING SKILLS:

According to research and studies, most people get almost the same score every time they take standardized tests if they don't do anything different to improve their skills. In other words, if you take your test over and over again without any additional effective effort to prepare yourself, your score is likely to remain somewhat the same each time, with a variation of 5% or less.

So, if you have taken your test many times and you are still getting almost the same score, obviously you are doing something wrong. You need to stop taking the test repeatedly, sit down, think, and analyze. You are probably doing something wrong, or your approach is wrong, or you are lacking some important skills. You need to correct these things first, before taking the test again. There is no point in taking the test without being completely prepared. It is always better to first fix the problem and then take the test instead of blindly taking the test in the hope that some miracle might happen and you'll get a better score without making the necessary effort. You should already know that nothing in life comes easy without making an effort and this is no exception. Think of the test as a warlike situation. It's better to be well equipped with all the tools, weapons, and ammunition and then go to war.

MOST COMMON DEFICIENCIES AND HOW TO OVERCOME THEM:

#1: LACK OF INTEREST IN THE SUBJECT:
Deficiency: Lack of interest in the subject can affect how you approach the test and prepare yourself. It is the number one cause of not being able to concentrate or understand your material. It is very important to develop an interest in the subject in order to do well. If you have an interest in the subject, it will be easier for you to understand the material, and you will be more likely to perform better. If you enjoy what you are working on, then it's not considered work. For instance, if you are a big fan of music, all the names on top of the charts will be on the tip of your tongue. Likewise, if you start enjoying what you study, you will easily be able to comprehend and retain the information. Remember, if you are interested in something, you are much more likely to learn faster and perform better.
Overcome: The best way to overcome this problem is by trying to develop an interest in the test subjects. Try to make the entire test preparation process a little more interesting and a little less boring. There are a variety of ways to make the test-prep more interesting, such as by making flash cards, asking a friend to quiz you, joining study groups, etc.

#2: LACK OF BACKGROUND KNOWLEDGE:
Deficiency: Lack of background knowledge can affect how you approach the test and prepare yourself. This can prevent your understanding about a particular subject. Learning is a step by step process, and it is often difficult to understand step 7 without knowing steps 1-6. It's like trying to climb the seventh step without going through the first six steps. You are bound to fall on your face.
Overcome: The best way to overcome this problem is by starting from scratch and acquiring those skills that are prerequisites for understanding what you are studying. For instance, if you have to learn how to simultaneously solve two linear equations in algebra and you don't even know the basics of algebra, it will be almost impossible for you to do it. So what you should do is start by learning basic algebra first, then simple equations, then linear equations, and then finally two linear equations. Therefore, make sure you have proper background knowledge about the various subjects. You can learn all the background information about all sections of the test by going through our books because in all our books, we start from scratch and we assume that you have no prior knowledge about the subject matter.

#3: LACK OF TEST-TAKING SKILLS:
Deficiency: Lack of test-taking skills can affect how you approach the test and prepare yourself. You may know the content but sometimes lack of test-taking skills can prevent you from choosing the correct answer.
Overcome: The best way to overcome this problem is by studying the test-taking skills given in this and our other books. Learning our exclusive test skills will definitely improve your odds of choosing the correct answer and your overall performance on standardized tests.

#4: LACK OF PROPER READING AND STUDY SKILLS:
Deficiency: Lack of proper reading and study skills can affect how you approach the test and prepare yourself. You must have proper basic reading skills to be able to prepare yourself for the test. Reading skills are difficult to master over a short period of time and are often developed over a long period of time.
Overcome: The best way to overcome this problem is by reading a lot of books, newsmagazines, journals, and articles. Developing effective reading skills is a prerequisite to your test preparation and performance.

#5: LACK OF PROPER STUDY PLAN:

Deficiency: Lack of a proper study plan can affect how you approach the test and prepare yourself. No matter what you do in life, it is essential that you have a proper plan that you follow religiously. Lack of a proper and regular study plan can be the biggest cause of not being able to study and prepare yourself effectively for the test.

Overcome: The best way to overcome this problem is by trying to set and follow a routine, such as the same study period, time, and place every day. Keep all your study material at that place so you have a proper study environment. Developing such habits will help you condition and motivate your mind to study. For more details, we have made a seven-step study plan in a section later in this book. We highly recommend that you follow it and make some alterations if needed.

#6: LACK OF CONCENTRATION:

Deficiency: Lack of concentration can affect how you approach the test and prepare yourself. If you find yourself daydreaming or thinking about something other than what you are studying, you are probably suffering from poor concentration. Preparing yourself for the test requires a lot of studying and practice which will not be very effective if you are not able to concentrate. You may be studying very hard for long hours, but if you are not able to concentrate on what you are studying, then it defeats the whole purpose of studying.

Overcome: The best way to overcome this problem is to stop thinking of anything other than what you are studying. There are certain fertile breeding grounds for poor concentration. If there is something that you need to take care of, simply note it down on a piece of paper so that you can do it later. If you still can't stop yourself from thinking about those other things, it may be better that you first take care of what you are thinking, and then get back to your books. You must develop and build your concentration skills so that you are able to comprehend and understand your material quickly.

#7: LACK OF SUFFICIENT TIME:

Deficiency: Lack of sufficient time can affect how you approach the test and prepare yourself. There are no shortcuts to success in life. Likewise, there are no shortcuts to success on your test. In order to be adequately prepared and do well on the test, you need to spend the required time.

Overcome: The best way to overcome this problem is by investing time into your test; there is simply no way of getting around it. Some students may have to spend more time than others, but the bottom line is that we all have to invest appropriate time to achieve something in life. Therefore, you should plan ahead how much time each day or week you need to spend in order to accomplish your goals.

#8: LACK OF FIRM GOALS:

Deficiency: Lack of firm goals can affect how you approach the test and prepare yourself. Goals are standards toward which your endeavors should be directed. Without goals, there will be no direction for your endeavors. Lack of goals is similar to traveling without having any clue of your destination. Doing something without any goals or targets is like wandering in the desert without knowing in which direction to go.

Overcome: The best way to overcome this problem is by setting realistic and achievable goals so that you have a sense of direction. You should set goals for each study session, each chapter, each section, each practice exercise, each practice test, and finally for the actual test. Next, you should make every effort in order to make sure that you are able to accomplish your goals or even exceed them.

#9: LACK OF ENERGY:

Deficiency: Lack of energy can affect how you approach the test and prepare yourself. Preparing for a test is nothing like wrestling or running a marathon; however, you do need a considerable level of mental, physical, and emotional energy to do well on your test. You can't afford to get tired, fatigued, or experience sleepiness while studying or taking the test.

Overcome: The best way to overcome this problem is by increasing your energy level by exercising, having a healthy diet, taking proper rest, and sleeping enough hours.

#10: LACK OF PROPER STUDY CONDITIONS:

Deficiency: Lack of proper study conditions can affect how you approach the test and prepare yourself. It is important to have proper study conditions in order to best prepare yourself for the test.

Overcome: The best way to overcome this problem is by keeping your study place comfortable, and free from any type of disturbances and distractions.

#11: LACK OF MOTIVATION:

Deficiency: Lack of motivation can affect how you approach the test and prepare yourself. It's human psychology that one needs to be motivated toward what one needs to accomplish. If you are not motivated enough to do well on your test, chances are that you will not do well on the test. Studying half-heartedly will not take you too far.

Overcome: The best way to overcome this problem is by motivating yourself to do well on your test. Think about why you want to take this test and make a list of the benefits of getting a good score on the test.

#12: LACK OF PEACE OF MIND:

Deficiency: Lack of peace of mind can affect how you approach the test and prepare yourself. It is important that you have peace of mind while studying for the test.

Overcome: The best way to overcome this problem is by keeping your mind stressfree and worryfree. Don't worry about personal problems or about your performance while you are studying.

2.8: REVIEWING TIPS:

While reviewing the material, you should apply the following points for most effective results:

(A) Highlight Key Terms: You should highlight key terms and information by highlighting, underlining, and/or circling.

(B) Make Notes – Summary Sheets: It is essential that you make your own notes on the summary sheets on all the key concepts in your own style. This can prove to be useful since writing and then reading what you wrote is an excellent way of understanding and retaining information. Make one sheet for each chapter or topic that outlines and consolidates all of its important concepts, terms, and formulas in a condensed and organized manner. Also, make one summary of all the summary sheets, which will be your master summary sheet. This process may take some time, but it will be time well spent. You can use these study sheets periodically throughout your study plan and the day before your test date for a brush up.

Things to keep in mind while taking quality notes:

- Your notes should be precise and concise.
- It is also a good idea to organize your notes by outlining, drawing diagrams, charts, flow charts, etc, for visual aid.
- Emphasize important points by listing, underlining, highlighting, capital letters, asterisks, stars, circles, etc.
- Make references when a topic corresponds to pages in the text – include those page numbers in the notes to refer back to when studying if needed.
- Use the white space on the paper properly. Maintain approximately 1-inch margins. Separate main topics by drawing a thick line. Use columns if needed.
- Define difficult vocabulary – check for a glossary in the book or look for the definition in the text and add this to your notes.
- For fast paced lectures, use abbreviations.
- Your notes should display lists of important information in a hierarchical manner.
- Creativity and a visual framework will help you recall these ideas.

(C) Use Index/Flash Cards: You can also use index cards to help you in memorizing the important facts and concepts. Use one index card for each topic and condense all your notes on the key facts and concepts into it.

- Put words to be learned on one side of the index card and a subject matter definition on the other side. Practice by reading the definitions and then by reading the words. The same holds good for formulas.
- Create flashcards for definitions, formulas, or lists that you need to have memorized put topics on one side of the card, and answers on the other. You can later use those index cards in random order, to test yourself, or ask one of your friends to give you a quiz on the key facts and concepts. Flashcards will not only enable you to test your ability to recognize important information, but also your ability to retrieve information from scratch.

(D) Use Supplemental Material: You can review your references and sources. You can also use any other supplemental material provided for the test-prep.

(E) Review Everything: Anticipate what is more likely to be on the test, based on prior tests, study guides, and feedback from other students who have taken the same test in the past. Get as much information as you can about the test. But don't leave any stones unturned – review everything completely.

(F) Use Audio Aids: Record your notes so you can review material walking or relaxing in a nonacademic environment.

(G) Create Study Checklists: Identify all of the material that you will need for your test – list notes, formulas, ideas, and text assignments, etc. This checklist will enable you to break up your studying into organized, manageable chunks, which will allow you to have a comprehensive review plan.

By now, you should have a structured and organized outline detailing all the key facts and concepts.

2.9: HOW TO TAKE PRACTICE TESTS:

SIMULATE REAL TEST-TAKING CONDITIONS:

While taking practice tests, you should try to duplicate and replicate the test conditions as close to those of the real test as possible. Please note the following points while taking practice tests:

(A) Quiet Place Free of Distractions, Disturbances, or Interruptions: You should sit down in a quiet place where you can work with full concentration. Your study place must be free from any sort of distractions, interruptions or disturbances, such as from television, radio, phone, pets, etc. during the time you take the practice test.

(B) Do Not Use Outside Assistance: Do not use any outside assistance since that could very seriously hamper your own efforts. If you use any outside assistance such as referring to your book or notes – your practice test score may not truly reflect your abilities or indicate your performance.

(C) Timed Conditions: While taking a full-length practice test, make sure that you strictly observe the time limits established for each test-section, and that you do not allow yourself any more time than what you would get on the actual test. It is recommended that you use a stop watch to time yourself. You can start off by setting the timer of the stop watch for the time that is allotted to each section of the test, and make sure to reset it for the appropriate amount of time whenever you start a new section. Please note that different sections may have different time limits. Time yourself accurately, preferably with the same device and in the same manner in which you plan to keep track of your time during the actual test.

If you fall into the habit of taking as much time on the practice test-sections as you like, and/or use any outside assistance, you will be sabotaging your own efforts, as none of these would help you on the actual test. If you use more time in taking the practice test than needed – your practice test score may not truly reflect your abilities or indicate your performance.

Remember, this test does not only assess your ability to answer the questions correctly; instead, it measures your ability to answer the questions correctly in the given amount of time as well.

(D) Mark Your Answers on the Answer Sheet, Not on your Book or Test Booklet: You should carefully tear out the answer sheet provided with each practice-test and mark your answer with a pencil, just like you would on the actual test. According to the research and studies we have conducted, for the multiple choice tests, it does take slightly longer to work through a test by filling the answers in a separate answer sheet rather than merely circling your chosen answers in the practice test book or the test booklet. Since this is how you would have to answer on your actual test, following the same method of marking your answers will make you get more accustomed to the real test-taking conditions. For the essay section, you should use your own lined paper for each practice essay test. But make sure you allow yourself the same amount of space as you would be allowed on the actual test, which is normally two pages, the front and the back of a single sheet of paper.

(E) Take One Part of the Practice Test at a Time: In the beginning, it is not a good idea that you take all the sections of the practice test in one sitting, instead you should take one part of the practice test at a time. For instance, take only the math or the verbal sections of the practice test in one sitting. Taking the complete set of a practice test in one sitting may lead to loss of concentration or fatigue. After taking a couple of practice tests in different parts, you should start taking full length practice tests in one sitting, just like you would in an actual test.

(F) Take the Practice Test at the Same Time of Day as your Actual Test: For some individuals, when and where they perform a certain task can make a difference. Hence, you should try to take the full-length practice test at the same time of day as your actual test, as if it were the real test day.

Source: The best source for taking full-length practice tests is the one provided by the test administrator, either in a hardcopy book version or an online version available on their website.

Advantages of Following Real Test-Taking Conditions: There are numerous advantages of following the real test-taking conditions while taking your practice test.

- If you cannot finish all the test questions in a particular test section in time, you will know that you need to work faster and increase your speed. Conversely, if you finish all the test questions in a particular test section before the allotted time is up, you will know that you need to work slower, and perhaps you can afford to spend more time on each question and double-check to make sure you get the correct answer.

- You will also come to know your strengths and weaknesses, and accordingly you can augment your strengths and hopefully eliminate your weaknesses by reinforcing those skills.
- Also, try not to worry too much about your scores or about whether you get a specific question right or wrong.
- The practice tests don't count; however, they are an excellent source for examining your performance and determining how you can get through each one better and faster on an actual test.

Strictly Adhere to the Abovementioned Real Test-Taking Conditions: Remember the whole purpose of taking the practice tests would be defeated if you do not strictly adhere to the abovementioned real test-taking conditions. Your scores can be very misleading and you will not get an accurate idea of how well you did on your practice test, if you allow yourself more time than the actual test, and/or use any outside assistance.

See if You are Able to Complete the Test on Time: If you were not able to answer all the questions and finish your test in the allotted time, you should try to improve your speed so that you can finish the test on time the next time you take it.

REVIEW PRACTICE TESTS:

(A) Score Your Practice Test: After completing each test, refer to the answer keys to score your test. Carefully identify your correct and incorrect answers. If you take an online version, the score will be automatically compiled for you.

(B) Analyze Your Practice Tests: Taking the practice tests will give you good practice of the real test and evaluating them thoroughly will tell you where you stand. Moreover, analyzing them will dramatically help you in identifying your strengths and weaknesses, monitoring your performance, thereby making you a smarter test-taker. All this will further prepare you for your next practice test and ultimately for the upcoming actual test. This is a good opportunity to find out what you don't understand and this is the time to correct any testing deficiencies that you may have. You can also use your tests to review when studying for your actual test.

(C) Study the Detailed Explanatory Answers to all the Questions: You should thoroughly review the detailed explanatory answers to all the questions that you answered correctly, incorrectly, or omitted, and study the appropriate review material continuously until you are confident that you completely understand the concepts, strategies, and philosophies behind these materials. You should concentrate on reviewing your difficult areas where you need more help so that you are able to overcome your weaknesses. Review and concentrate on one test section at a time.

- **(i) Study the Detailed Explanatory Answers to the Questions You Get Right:** Make sure you get the correct answer for the right reasons.
- If you realize that you got some of the questions right because you guessed them and got lucky, study the answer explanations to those questions and learn how to answer them correctly. Also, go back to the related review sections, and study and reinforce those skills again.
- You may also realize that although you got the correct answers to some of the questions, there might be an easier and quicker method of answering the same questions correctly. Learn those easier and quicker methods to save yourself some valuable time on your next test.
- **(ii) Study the Detailed Explanatory Answers to the Questions You Got Wrong:** Figure out why you missed certain questions. Study the detailed explanatory answers to those questions and learn how to answer them correctly. Also, go back to the related review sections and study and reinforce those skills again.
- **(iii) Study the Detailed Explanatory Answers to the Questions You Omitted:** Figure out why you were not able to answer these questions. Study the detailed explanatory answers to those questions and learn how to answer them correctly. Also, go back to the related review sections and study and reinforce those skills again.
- **(iv) Look for a Pattern of Errors and Make a Systematic List of Your Strengths & Weaknesses:** Look for a pattern in the questions you get right, wrong or have omitted. Make a systematic list of those questions and topics. This may indicate your strengths and weaknesses. You must prepare for all question types; however, concentrate on your weak areas where you feel less confident, and reinforce your strong areas where you already have an edge.

(D) Review your Weak and Strong Areas: Make sure to review your weak as well as strong areas.
- **(i) Weak Areas:** Go back to those weak areas and review those sections so that you don't make the same mistake again. For instance, your list may indicate that you are missing a lot of questions that involve percentages, or ratios, or subject-verb agreements, or parallelisms, etc. You should go back, review, and

reinforce those specific areas once again, and make sure that you understand and master those skills completely. Doing so will help you avoid making the same mistakes again.

(ii) Strong Areas: Make sure not to ignore your strong areas. In fact, cash in on your strengths and this is where you'll rack up most of the valuable points.

Weak to Strong and Strong to Stronger: At the end, you must minimize your weak points and convert them to strong points. Also, make your strong points even stronger.

Keep Track of Your Test Scores: Keep track of your scores on each practice test. This is necessary to monitor changes in your performance from test to test, and to be able to perform better in each subsequent practice test.

REPEAT THE SAME PROCEDURE AFTER TAKING EACH PRACTICE TEST:

Repeat the above procedure after taking each practice test. Do not take the next practice test until you review the previous practice test, go through the explanatory answers, and study the relevant review sections. You should learn from your mistakes, work on your weaknesses, and then move on to the next practice test. Make sure that you don't make the same mistakes again and that you are able to overcome your weaknesses. Making a mistake once is understandable, but making it repeatedly is not acceptable. In other words, do everything that you can to improve your performance for the next test.

2.10: STUDY GROUPS:

THE STUDY GROUP PROGRAM:
Some people study more effectively alone and some in a group, but by and large, studying in a group has a lot of benefits. Remember, two heads are better than one. To make the best use of your group time, your group must agree on a standard procedure for learning. Note that these are general guidelines and you may need to iron them out to fit your individual study needs. If you think group study is right for you, use the following helpful tips.

ORGANIZE A STUDY GROUP:
- It is always a good idea to form study groups with a few conscientious friends/colleagues.
- Meet with the same group consistently throughout your study plan.

PROVIDE OR SEEK:
Each member of the group must know their strengths and weaknesses so that they can "provide" help or "seek" assistance among themselves.

BENEFITS OF A STUDY GROUP:
You may not be a group person but there are some distinctive advantages of studying in a group that can't be ignored, such as the ones given below:
- Accomplish more by sharing each other's skills and resources instead of working alone.
- Quiz each other on important materials.
- Share other people's perspectives, thoughts, and understanding about a particular topic; the more you can offer to the group, the more you'll get out of it.
- Compare and share notes so that you can learn new information that you may have overlooked on your own.
- While in a study group environment, just to save your reputation, you are far less likely to blow it off if you know that your friends are depending on you to show up at meetings and being productive.
- Sometimes, it's hard to see your own weaknesses, while others can. Your group members can point out your faults, and if you're lucky, they'll even help you work on your trouble spots. As you may already know, some people take pride in pointing out other people's mistakes. If that ever happens to you, don't take it personally; instead, make the best use of their criticism. If you are really serious about learning, then criticism can prove to be both constructive and beneficial.
- One man's loss is another man's gain – you can also learn from other members' mistakes. So, in this case, "mistakes" mean "learning."
- The competitive nature of a group setting will not only keep you on your toes and help you motivate yourself, but will also provide you with a consistent support system.

PICKING GROUP MEMBERS WISELY:
- Pick group members who can actually help you get prepared for the test. You don't have to team up with straight-A students. You should also try to avoid students who are far below your level. Instead, choose people who are more or less at the same level of ability as you are. At least, few of them should be at your level and a few better than you.
- Make sure that all the members of your study group are serious about studying and doing well on the test. Stay away from people who are not as serious as you are about preparing for the test as that may lead to wasting your precious study time. In general, avoid people who aren't serious about working and/or who raise your anxiety level.

NUMBER OF GROUP MEMBERS:
- An ideal group size would be six to eight members.
- Having the right number of group members is also important. You should not have so few members that there is hardly any interaction, or so many that you feel crowded. Doing so will let the group reap all the benefits of teaming up, and at the same time, there will be a healthy interaction and no one will get overshadowed or feel left out.

MAKE IRONCLAD SCHEDULE:

- Make an ironclad schedule on a calendar for the entire group for the dates, times, and the material to be covered. Every group member must mark down every meeting in advance and commit to those times.
- Ideally, try to schedule four to six meetings per week, each of at least one to two hours. It will be hard to accomplish much in less time than this.

PICKING A MEETING PLACE:

- You must pick an appropriate and convenient (to all group members) meeting place for your group. Fix a constant meeting place for each meeting and try not to change your meeting place for every meeting.
- In order to optimize your group study time, your group meeting place must be comfortable, spacious, and free from any distractions.
- Some good examples of ideal study spots would be a library group meeting room, a group member's dining room table, or any other quiet and comfortable place in your school/office/home.
- It may be a good idea to have some light snacks and beverages to boost spirits and energy levels.

APPOINT A GROUP LEADER:

- Having one person act as the leader can help a group run smoothly and effectively.
- The main goal of the leader is to keep everyone focused on studying so the environment doesn't become too social.

Rotation: It may be a good idea to rotate the group leader. One way to do so would be to appoint a different group leader for each session so that every member gets an equal opportunity to lead the group. If your study material is divided into units, an effective way would be to pick a group leader for each unit or chapter. For every subsequent group session, appoint your group leader for the next session in advance. Every other member must review the material ahead of time, but it is the responsibility of the group leader to set up the agenda for the rest of the group for that session. There are many advantages of following this process. It takes a lot of preparation and planning to lead the group, and the person who is leading the session should master that material really well. It also keeps everyone active. Another exciting idea would be to appoint your group leader right at the beginning of each session. Since any one of the group members can be picked as the leader for that session, everyone would be prepared in advance to lead the group, unless they want other members to think they are sloppy!

IF YOU CAN TEACH OTHERS, YOU KNOW IT DARNED WELL:

Try to teach what you learned to your other group members; if you can teach others then you can be sure that you know the material and understand it well enough. This will also add other people's perspectives and help to complete your study just in case you missed some important topics.

SET REALISTIC GROUP GOALS:

You must have individual goals; however, since you are working in a group environment, it's important to have a few group goals so that the group can head in the same general direction and work well together.

2.11: UNDERSTAND THE TEST:

HOW STANDARDIZED TESTS ARE CONSTRUCTED AND HOW TO CRACK THEM:

The best way to crack the test is by understanding how it is constructed. You must understand how a test is put together if you want to rip it apart.

Standardized tests use the same standards to measure students' performances across the country. Everyone takes the same test according to the same rules. This makes it possible to measure each student's performance against that of others. The group with whom a student's performance is compared is a "norm group" and consists of many students of the same age or grade who take the same test.

Although various standardized tests have some differences, they all test the same fundamental knowledge, i.e. arithmetic, algebra, geometry, vocabulary, reading comprehension, grammar, writing skills – in a slightly different way, i.e. problem solving, quantitative comparison, data sufficiency, sentence correction, sentence completion, critical reading, critical reasoning, etc.

Most standardized tests are straightforward skill tests. They test you on how much of the required skills you know and how well you can apply that information in different situations. Standardized tests require you to interpret questions, analyze situations, synthesize material, and apply specific knowledge to specific questions. Every standardized test is based on psychometrics, the peculiar science concerned with creating "standardized" tests. To do well on standardized tests, you need to understand the science on which the test is formulated.

In order for a test to be categorized as a "standardized test," it must have the following characteristics:
(A) **Reliability:** The test must have a high score reliability; meaning, a particular test-taker who takes the test should get approximately the same score if he or she takes it over again (assuming, that the person didn't go through any major test-prep program such as the EZ Solutions test-prep set of books between the two tests.)
(B) **Similarity:** The test must contain the same basic concepts each time it is designed with only some stylistic changes.
(C) **Mediocrity:** When the test is given to a diversified group of people, some will do very well, and some will do very poorly, but the great majority will score somewhere in the middle. If you plot all these test scores, you will form a bell-curve type of graph, where the heavy concentration is towards the middle.

Norming: Standardizes tests use a process known as norming to construct other tests. How this works is, they take a "normed" test and a "revised" test and give it to a large diversified group of people. If most students in that group get almost consistent scores in both tests, then the "revised" test is just as valid and consistent as the "normed" test. This is done exhaustively to ensure statistical validity. This process is known as norming, and this is how most standardized tests are constructed.

Predictability and Coachability: The basic foundation upon which standardized tests are constructed makes it the most predictable test. And, the "predictable" nature of standardized tests is what makes them extremely "coach-able." The characteristics of standardized tests make it easy to crack because of the following reasons:
- Since standardized tests must be "reliable," the test is highly set in its format and style. This means, we can tell you every nut and bolt of the test in advance so that there will not be any surprises.
- Since standardized tests must be "similar," they test the same concepts in each and every test, again and again, with subtle variations. This means, we can tell you what's going to be on the test and what's not going to be on the test so that you can better prepare yourself.
- Since standardized tests must have "mediocrity" and form a bell-curve, the test must contain some questions that most test-takers will always get right, some questions that most test-takers will always get wrong, and some questions that most test-takers will get right some of the times and wrong the other times. This means you'll see some common traps and we'll teach you how to recognize these traps and not get tricked.

We have it all covered for you, our objective is to tell you everything about how standardized tests are constructed and what you need to know in order to crack them.

SALIENT CHARACTERISTICS OF STANDARDIZED TESTS:

Standardized tests are quite different from most school tests, and you must take advantage of their peculiar structure by learning about how they're designed.

Remember the following things about standardized tests:

- All questions, easy or difficult, are worth equal points (except on CAT).
- You earn points for a correct answer, and not how you approach a question or reach the correct answer.

Hence, while taking a standardized test, your primary objective should be to score as many points as you can within the given timeframe. It's that simple, and you will learn everything you need, right here in this book.

2.12: UNDERSTAND THE TEST MAKER'S PHILOSOPHY:

It would be very helpful for you as a test-taker to get into the mind of the test makers and understand their philosophy. Your test-taking strategies must be able to anticipate the test maker's fabricated tricks. You should be able to understand the test maker's thinking process. Also, you must understand what kind of difficulties test makers go through while constructing the test, so that you can make a plan on how to overcome those difficulties. To properly understand how the test maker's mind works, you should ask yourself, what you would do to make some incorrect answer choices.

PLAY THE ROLE OF A DETECTIVE:
For every question, you should try to play the role of Sherlock Holmes, the detective, in which you adopt an investigative approach and doubt every possibility unless you are completely sure. By adopting this approach, you will not fall in the test maker's trap and will evaluate each alternative until you are certain.

THINK LIKE A TEST MAKER:
For multiple choice sections, the test maker has to first formulate a unique question and the correct answer, which is fairly easy. Then, he has to come up with 3-4 incorrect answer choices for every correct answer, which can often be much more difficult than it appears. There are obviously multiple ways to make those 3-4 incorrect answer choices. But the test maker would not like to make those 3-4 incorrect answer choices so obviously wrong that no one would ever choose them. It would be pointless to make incorrect answer choices if no one will ever pick them. The test makers want to make incorrect answer choices in such a way so that they look appealing and tempting, and can work as effective distracters from the correct answers. The test makers like to throw in some bait to make the incorrect answer choices look correct.

TRICK OF THE TEST:
Some questions on the tests may seem tricky, and it's sometimes difficult to discern what a convoluted question is asking for or how to choose among somewhat similar answer choices. The fact is that the questions on the test are not intentionally written to deceive you. There is probably something that you are still not able to understand in the question and it is preventing you from seeing the differences in the answer choices. Re-read the question, use all your knowledge, common sense, experience, test-taking skills, and then choose the best answer.

MOST COMMON DISTRACTERS:
Following are some of the most common test maker's tactics for making the distracters:
- Overstate or exaggerate the point.
- Ignore the fine points.
- Change just one detail and keep everything else the same.
- Keep some exact words from the "fact pattern" in the incorrect answer choices.
- Make a two-part answer choice that is partly correct – the answer choice may have two parts, one of which is correct and the other is incorrect. The answer choice may start with something that is correct and then later has something that makes the whole statement incorrect.
- Twist the meaning around.
- Include double negatives.

2.13: EZ SEVEN STEP STUDY PLAN:

MAP OUT AN EFFECTIVE STUDY PLAN:
Your mission should be to do well on your test, and like any other mission in life, this one too should have a plan. It is always better to have a plan, rather than just working haphazardly. We recommend you follow our "EZ Seven Step Study Plan", listed in this section, which should help you to achieve your goals. Feel free to modify or alter it according to your specific needs. You must approach your test strategically, actively, and tactfully.

STEP 1: FIND OUT THE DETAILS ABOUT THE TEST:
The very first thing you should do is to find out thoroughly each and every up-to-date test detail that you should know in order to better prepare yourself for the test. It would be hard to do anything without having all the relevant information. Find out things like, how many sections does the test have, what types of questions are in each section, total number of questions, total test time, etc.

STEP 2: TAKE A DIAGNOSTIC TEST: GET TO KNOW WHERE YOU STAND:
Your first step towards preparing for the test is to take a diagnostic test. The sample test itself will be a good way to learn what to expect on the real test. Your score will be an important indicator of telling you where you stand and what you need to do in order to reach your target score. By doing so, you will be able to find out about your strengths and weaknesses. You can accordingly make your strengths stronger and weaknesses weaker by reinforcing those skills. You should also carefully review the explanations for all the questions. You may find an easier and quicker way to answer the same question that you already answered correctly, and also learn how to answer the question correctly that you get wrong. It is always better to first do a diagnosis, and then treat the problem.

STEP 3: REVIEW MATERIAL: THOROUGHLY LEARN & REVIEW ALL THE CONCEPTS IN EACH TEST SECTION:
Your second step towards preparing for the test is to thoroughly and effectively review all the concepts for each test-section presented in our books. Review at your own pace, work as slowly as is necessary for you to absorb and understand the material thoroughly. Make connections between concepts, and then draw conclusions. You may have to spend relatively more time in your weak areas than your strong areas. It's fine if you choose to spend less time in your strong areas, but do not completely skip the areas you think you are already good at; always remember, it never hurts to reinforce your skills or knowledge.

Review & Understand the Material, and Also Learn How to Apply the Concepts in Real Time: It's very important for you to review and understand each concept, but it is even more important for you to know how to apply those concepts in the actual test questions for most effective results. Just learning the concepts and not understanding how to apply them in the actual test questions would be a job half done. Therefore, make sure that you not only review and understand the material, but also know how to apply it in real time.
- Develop a study plan which allows plenty of time for reviewing all the material.
- Organize material so that the most important material will be given the greatest amount of time.

"Over Study" – Repeat, Reinforce, Re-review: Review at least more than once. The more effort and energy you put into learning, the more likely you'll do well on the test. Studying and learning can never be enough. Study as much as you can and gain as much knowledge as you can to have a strong grip on your test. Study so much that the material gets into your veins and the content of your test becomes the law of nature, of course, metaphorically speaking.

STEP 4: LEARN TEST-TAKING STRATEGIES: BECOME A SMARTER TEST-TAKER:
Your next step towards preparing for the test is to learn our test-taking strategies. You may be very good in some of the areas, but it does not mean that you are an expert in answering questions asked in those areas. Some people think that they are experts in the content and can ace the test, but that does not always prove to be true.

There is a fine line between being an expert in the contents and being an expert test-taker. Both skills are different from one another and both skills are equally important to understand. To do well on the test and get a good score, make sure that you acquire both of these skills; you can't do well with just one without the other.

There are a lot of test-taking strategies listed in our books which will make you a smart test-taker. Make sure you take advantage of them by learning them ahead of time. The test maker makes the test tricky, and we tell you how to crack them with our proven test-taking strategies.

STEP 5: TAKE PRACTICE EXERCISES: PRACTICE THE SKILLS YOU JUST LEARNED:

Your next step towards preparing for the test is to complete each and every practice exercise after you finish each topic area. Apply what you learned in those practice exercises. Review the explanations for each question you answered incorrectly. If you don't feel confident about a particular topic, go back and review it again until you master it.

STEP 6: TAKE PRACTICE TESTS: GET ACCUSTOMED TO REAL TEST-TAKING CONDITIONS.

Take the timed, full-length practice tests to become better at test-taking, managing your time, monitoring your progress, and gauging your endurance. Athletes, actors, musicians, and dancers practice and rehearse for hours. When performers are on stage, their anxiety is channeled into focused energy. Practice taking sample tests and you will be more confident during the actual test.

STEP 7: FINAL BRUSH UP: DO A FINAL BRUSH UP AND MAKE SURE YOU ARE READY TO TAKE THE ACTUAL TEST.

You should do a final brush up by touching up with the summary sheets and flash cards that you had prepared while reviewing. By this time, you should be at the end of your study plan and be ready to take the actual test. Do not allow a long gap between the time you finish your study plan and your actual test. Since all the information that you learned is fresh in your mind, it is recommended that you should take the test right after you complete your study plan. Strike the iron while it's hot!

Note: Before you move on to the next step, make sure you have successfully completed the previous step(s).

PART 3.0: WHAT, HOW, AND WHEN ABOUT TEST CENTER:

TABLE OF CONTENTS:

THIS PAGE HAS BEEN INTENTIONALLY LEFT BLANK.

3.1: WHAT ARE THE RULES & REGULATIONS OF THE TEST CENTER:

THINGS YOU CAN/CAN'T TAKE TO THE TEST CENTER:

THINGS YOU NEED TO TAKE TO THE TEST CENTER:

Following is a list of some of the things that you should take with you to the test center on the test day:

(A) **Admission Ticket:** Take your admission ticket for the paper-and-pencil test and/or your authorization voucher/number appointment for the computer-based test.

Note: Depending on how you register for your test, sometimes you may not be provided with an authorization voucher; instead, you'll be assigned a confirmation number by which you can identify yourself to the test center staff. Make sure to have that number with you on the day of the test.

(B) **Proper ID:** On the day when you take the test, you will be asked to present an acceptable ID. Your ID must be current and contain the following:

- Your name – exactly as provided when you scheduled your test appointment.
- A recent, recognizable photograph.
- Your signature.

Acceptable ID's: Driver's license, or state ID, or passport, or military ID with a photo and a signature.

Unacceptable ID's: Note that any expired ID's, credit cards of any kind, social security card, international driver's license, international student ID, notary-prepared letter or document, employee ID card, photocopy of ID, birth certificates, learner's permit or any temporary identification documents (e.g., driver's license) will not be accepted.

Note: Make sure your identifying information, such as name, address, etc, is correct and it matches exactly what's on your admission ticket. If there are any errors in the information on your admission ticket, you must get it corrected before you take the test. If your ID does not include all the above mentioned elements, or if the test administrator has any reason to question the validity of your ID, you will be required to present an additional ID. You will not be admitted inside the test center if you do not have proper identification. For security reasons, if the name on your ID does not match the name on your admission ticket or test appointment, the test administrator has the right to turn you away from the test center, not allowing you to take the test. ID verification at the test center may include thumb-printing, photographing, videotaping, or any other form of electronic ID confirmation methods. If you refuse to participate, you will not be permitted to take the test and your test fee will be forfeited.

(C) **Pencils:** Take plenty of well-sharpened No. 2 pencils (at least five) if you are taking the paper-based test.

(D) **Erasers:** Take a couple of new erasers that erase cleanly and do not leave a mark/residue upon erasing if you are taking the paper-based test.

(E) **Accurate Watch:** Take a watch (without beep/alarm) to keep track of time and to help you pace yourself better. Although, most test rooms will have wall clocks and the test supervisor will announce when there are 5 minutes remaining on each individual test section, it's good to be self reliant with your own personal reliable watch.

(F) **Snack/Beverage:** Take a light snack like a fruit or an energy-bar to keep your energy up for the later sections of the test. Also keep a bottle of water and a light beverage for a quick boost at break time. You'll probably get thirsty and/or hungry during the course of the test.

Note: Food/drinks are only allowed during break time; they are strictly prohibited in the test room.

(G) **Painkiller:** Take aspirin or some other painkiller, just in case you get a headache or body-ache.

(H) **Calculator:** Keep in mind the following (only if you are allowed to use a calculator during the test):

- Your calculator must be one of the acceptable ones.
- Your calculator should have fresh batteries.
- You may use your calculator only during the math section.
- You may not share your calculator with anyone else.
- You may not store test material in your calculator's memory.

Note: Use a calculator you're familiar with when you take the math section. Using a more powerful/complex, but unfamiliar calculator is not likely to give you an advantage over the one that you normally use.

(I) **Score Recipients:** Names of schools which you'd like to send your scores to.

(J) **Eyeglasses/Contacts:** If you need to wear special glasses when you work at a computer or to read, make sure to keep them with you. If you wear contact lenses, it may also be a good idea to keep an extra pair of contact lenses and some rewetting drops for dry eyes.

Note: You must turn off your cell phone, pager, or any other electronic device that beeps or makes any type of noise so it won't disturb others. If any of your electronic gadgets go off during testing, you will be dismissed and your test will not be scored. Also, the test premises are subject to audio/video recording and other real-time monitoring, and strict rules about people and material entering and leaving the test facility are enforced.

BRING YOUR OWN WATCH TO THE TEST CENTER:

It would be advisable to bring a watch with you so that you can pay attention to the passing time. It would be even better if you have a stop watch or a digital watch. Make sure that your watch does not make any beep sounds. Even if there is a clock in the room, it is always better for you to have one on your desk.

(A) If you have a normal watch: Before you start each section of the test, set your watch to 12:00. It is easier to keep track of your time and know that a section is approaching its end as the time in the watch approaches 12:30. It would be a little bit more difficult to keep track of your time if you were to start a section at 8:57 and have to remember that it will be over at 9:27.

(B) If you have a stop-watch: It would be even easier if you have a digital stopwatch that you start at the beginning of each section; you can either let it count down from 30 or whatever the duration of that section is, to zero, or let it count up from 0 to 30 or whatever the duration of that section is, and know that your time will be up after those many or fewer minutes.

THINGS YOU CANNOT TAKE TO THE TEST CENTER:

Following is the list of things that you cannot take with you to the test center on the test day:

(A) Testing Aids: Dictionaries, translators, thesauruses, or any other testing aid.

(B) Reading Material: Books, pamphlets, notes, or any other reading material.

(C) Writing Material: Scratch paper, notebooks, or any other writing material.
Note: You may not bring your own scratch paper to the test, if the use of scratch paper is allowed, it will be provided by the test administrator.

(D) Measuring Instruments: Rulers, protractors, compasses, or any other measuring instrument.

(E) Writing Instruments: Ink pens, highlighters, or any other writing instrument.

(F) Electronic Devices: Notebook/Laptop computers, handheld PCs, Personal Data Assistants (PDAs), etc.

(G) Communicating Devices: Cellular phones, beepers, pagers, radios, earphones, etc.

(H) Special Watches: Stop watches or watches with beep, signal, alarm, calculator, or any other special function.

(I) Calculators: If calculators are allowed, you'll be allowed to bring only one of the acceptable calculators and have it on your desk only during the math section.

(J) Baggage: Briefcases, bags, or any other type of baggage.

Note: Personal items such as hats, scarves, gloves, jackets, and outerwear that are taken into the test room are subject to inspection by the test center staff before being admitted to the test room.

EZ TIP: Avoid sudden panic on the morning of your test. It would be a good idea to set out your test kit a day before or at least the night before the test so that you can have peace of mind and a worry-free good night's sleep. Also, it's probably best to take with you only the things you'll need for the test, anything else will just be in your way.

PROHIBITED BEHAVIOR AT THE TEST CENTER:

You will be dismissed and all your scores will be cancelled if you are found:

- Looking back or ahead at a test in the test booklet on which you are currently not working.
- Looking at another examinee's test booklet or answer document or computer screen.
- Giving or receiving assistance.
- Using a prohibited calculator, sharing a calculator with another examinee, or using a calculator on any test other than the mathematics test.
- Using any device to share or exchange information at any time during the test or during breaks.
- Attempting to remove test material, including test questions or answers, from the test room by any means.
- Using highlight pens, colored pens or pencils, scratch paper, notes, dictionaries, or other aids.
- Not following instructions or abiding by the rules of the test center.
- Exhibiting confrontational, threatening, or unruly behavior.
- Creating a disturbance or allowing an alarm or phone to sound in the test room.

Note: Friends and/or relatives are not allowed to be in contact with you while you are taking the test. Only authorized personnel are allowed to be in the test room while the test is in progress.

REASONS FOR DISMISSAL FROM A TEST CENTER:

Do not engage in any prohibited behavior at the test center or you will be dismissed and all your testing documents will be forfeited and your scores cancelled.

A test administrator is authorized to dismiss you from a test session and/or cancel your scores for actions such as, but not limited to:

- failing to provide acceptable identification.
- obtaining improper access to the test, a part of the test, or any information about the test.
- attempting to take the test for someone else or having someone else take the test for you.
- attempting to give or receive assistance.
- using and/or having any communication device, such as a cell phone in your possession during the test session or during scheduled breaks.
- using any aids in relation with the test, such as: cell phones, pagers, beepers, calculators, watch calculators, stereos or radios with headphones, watch alarms (including those with flashing lights or alarm sounds), stop watches, books, pamphlets, notes, rulers, ink pens, highlighter pens, dictionaries, translators, and any hand-held electronic or photographic devices.
- creating any sort of disturbance.
- communicating or discussing in any form with anyone except the test center staff.
- removing or attempting to remove test content from the test center, including scratch paper (if provided).
- attempting to disclose and/or reproduce any test content by any means (e.g., hard copy, verbally, electronically) to any person or entity.
- bringing a weapon or firearm into the test center facility.
- bringing/having food, drink, or tobacco into the test room.
- leaving the test room during the test without prior permission from the test administrator.
- taking excessive or extended unscheduled breaks during the test session.
- looking at, referring to, or working on any test, or test section, when not authorized to do so, or working after the time is up.
- leaving the test center facility during the test session or during breaks.
- tampering with a computer or any other device, supplies, or fixture in the testing facility.
- failing to follow any of the test administration regulations contained in the test bulletin, given by the test administrator, or otherwise specified in any test material.

The test center staff reserves the right to take all actions, including, but not limited to, barring you from future test and/or canceling your scores for failure to comply with test administration rules and regulations or the test administrator's directions. If your scores are cancelled due to violation of rules and regulations, they will not be reported and your fees will not be refunded.

Note: You may be required to sign a confidentiality statement at the test center before you begin the testing process. If you do not complete and sign the statement, you cannot take the test and your fees will be forfeited.

BREAK REQUESTS:
If you need to leave your test session at any time other than the scheduled breaks, raise your hand to call upon the test administrator. It is important that you obtain the test administrator's permission to leave the room during the test. You will be required to sign the test center log register before and after the test session and at any time you leave or reenter the test room for breaks or any other reasons. Please note that the timing of the section will not stop and any time lost cannot be made up.
Note: At any time during the test, if you have any problem due to any reason, such as a faulty test booklet or an error with your computer, and you need the administrator's help, raise your hand and someone will be available to assist you.

RETURN TESTING MATERIALS:
At the conclusion of the test, you must return all your testing material, such as the test booklet, answer sheet, and scratch paper (if any), to the test administrator. These materials are the property of the test administrator and you are not allowed to take them home with you.

WORK ON DESIGNATED SECTIONS:
During the actual test, you are allowed to work only on the section of the test that the test administrator designates and only for the time allotted. While you are working on a particular test section, you may not go back to an earlier section of the test or go forward to a new section of the test. The test administrator is authorized to dismiss you from the center for not following these rules.

3.2: HOW TO GET TO THE TEST CENTER:

MAP & DIRECTIONS TO THE TEST CENTER:

Locations of your test center may vary considerably. Your test center may be a local public school, community college, or a nearby university campus. Your test center can be located close by to where you live or you may need to walk a few blocks, or drive several hours, maybe even to an unfamiliar place. The surroundings may be quite familiar, or they may be uncomfortably new. Whatever is your situation, be certain to allow plenty of time and consider the following points:

(A) Get a Map and Directions: Make sure you have an accurate map and directions to the test center so that you don't get lost and are able to find your way to the test center. Also, find out exactly where your test site is, exactly how you're going to get there, and exactly how long it will take to get there. Find the easiest, quickest way to get to your test site.

(B) Visit the Test Site a Few Days Prior to the Test Date: If you are not familiar with the area where the test center is located, or if you are not good with directions, it may be worth your while to visit your test center a few days before the test date so that you don't get lost on the day of the test and you know what to expect. This will be particularly helpful if you are especially anxious. Moreover, visiting your test center beforehand is a good way to ensure that you don't get lost on the day of your test.

(C) Do a Test Run: Also do a test-run to the test center a few days before you take the test to find out how much time it will take you to reach the test center. If you'll be going by car, check out the traffic patterns. If you'll be using public transportation, figure out exactly how to get from the bus stop or the train station to the test center. Remember, if you do a test run on an afternoon and your test is in the morning, or you do a test run on a weekend and your test is on a weekday or vice versa – don't forget to factor in the rush hour traffic.

(D) Identify the Exact Building and the Room: Please note that your test center could be located in suites in skyscrapers, storefront locations in the middle of busy malls, or even in large college campuses. If it's a big campus, make sure that you know the exact location of the building, the exact location of the room where the test is going to take place, and any special instructions for finding the entrance on the weekends. Also, try to find out what the rooms are like, how the desks are set up, and so on, anything that you may think would be helpful to you. Sometimes, seeing the actual room where your test will be administered and taking notice of minute details – such as the type of chair and desk you'll be working on (or workstation), whether the room is likely to be hot or cold, etc – may help to make you feel more comfortable. It may even be helpful if you bring some practice material and do at least a section or two at the actual test location. Doing this may prove to be very helpful if you are suffering from test anxiety.

(E) Identify the Closest Parking Place: Also, make sure you know the closest parking lot/garage to your test center.

(F) Don't get Lost: Being lost while going to the test center can lead to anguish and nervousness, which can in turn seriously affect your performance on the test. Therefore, try to eliminate any or all surprises before you take the actual test, so that you feel comfortable without thinking too much about the surroundings and are able to concentrate on the test.

(G) Set a Back-Up Transportation System: Arrange for a backup transportation to the test center, just in case your car breaks down or you miss your bus/train. If you have a friend who is also taking the test, you should follow each other. In case your car breaks down on your way to the test, you could ride along with your friend and still arrive at the test center on time.

3.3: WHEN TO GET TO THE TEST CENTER:

BE PUNCTUAL: DON'T BE LATE & DON'T BE TOO EARLY:

(A) Reach a Little Early: Make sure you reach the test center about 20-30 minutes before the test begins. Give yourself adequate time to get to the test center. Arriving early will give you a moment to relax and reduce your anxiety. This brief time period will also boost your confidence, give you time to think positive thoughts and focus your mind, and a chance to get your thoughts together and relax. This will also help you get into a test alert and calm mode instead of a tense and anxious mode.

(B) Don't Reach Too Early: Reaching the test center too early can also agitate the already nervous test-takers because of waiting anxiety or anxiety from other test-takers.

(C) Don't be Late: Being late to the test center can completely throw you off the loop and it can lead to anguish and nervousness, which can in turn make your heart pound and stress will pump through your veins – all this can very seriously affect your performance on the test.

(D) Be Seated on Time: To be able to perform at your best, it is important to be relaxed and seated before the test begins.

(E) Extra Time for Emergencies: Also, be sure to allow yourself some extra time, at least 45 minutes, for mishaps or emergencies, such as road blockages, traffic snarls, road constructions, unexpected detours, mass transit delays, etc. Nothing will cause more anxiety than arriving to the test center just a few minutes late.

Therefore, reach the test center a few minutes before the test begins so that you are relaxed, and perform at your optimum potential!

Note: No one will be admitted into the test center after the test has begun. So, if you reach the test center after the test has started, you may not be allowed to take the test.

THIS PAGE HAS BEEN INTENTIONALLY LEFT BLANK.

PART 4.0: TEST ANXIETY:

TABLE OF CONTENTS:

THIS PAGE HAS BEEN INTENTIONALLY LEFT BLANK.

4.1: BASICS ABOUT TEST ANXIETY:

Doing well on standardized tests does not necessarily depend only on how much you know; in order to do well, you must also be in control – you must have a positive attitude, stay alert and focused, be confident not nervous, be careful not careless, and concentrate on your work. All these things can dramatically affect your performance on the test.

Adopt a sportsman's attitude – "win if you can, lose if you must, but do the best you can."

WHAT IS TEST ANXIETY?
Anxiety is something that most people feel before performing or executing a challenging task, the outcome of which may determine their abilities. Test anxiety is stress, directly related to testing situations. The term "test-anxiety" refers to the extreme/intense emotional reactions or feelings, which is nervousness, uneasiness and/or apprehension experienced before, during, or after a test because of concern, worry, or fear of the outcome. Test anxiety is an advanced form of heightened concern; it is a response to any situation associated with testing.

Test anxiety is defined as the anxious feeling or excessive worry about doing well on a test, and it can be disastrous and dangerous for you. A condition characterized by persistent anxiety in test situations can be severe enough to seriously interfere with performance. It is when you are so nervous about preparing or taking a test that you have difficulty planning, thinking, concentrating, and recalling previous knowledge. This stress is so excessive that it hinders a person's ability to prepare properly and take the test effectively. It is a cognitive concern over performances (worry), and subjective feelings of stress involving attention to physiological arousal reactions, such as increased heart rate, sweaty palms, an ache in the stomach, or dryness of the mouth.

WHY OVERCOME TEST ANXIETY?
Test anxiety is the number one barrier to performing well on tests. It is a learned response to stress. Test anxiety interferes with concentration and memory, making it difficult or impossible to recall previously memorized material and resulting in test performance that does not accurately reflect the test-taker's intelligence or the amount of effort spent preparing for the test. Often, the memorized material is recalled once the test is over and the student leaves the test room. One should reduce test anxiety when it begins to interfere with test performance. Test anxiety can interfere significantly with your academic accomplishment and impair confidence and self esteem. Since exams, tests, quizzes, tryouts, presentations, interviews, and performance reviews are all evaluations and part of life, it is worth your time to learn to overcome test anxiety.

WHO EXPERIENCES TEST ANXIETY?
Anxiety is something that everyone experiences to some extent in some form in any stressful situation. For most part, all students, or at least most students, at some point or the other, experience some level of tension and/or nervousness, commonly referred to as anxiety, before and while taking a test or any other important events in their lives. For some, it's within manageable means, and for others it becomes a serious test-taking problem, the one that they need to work and improve upon. If you are a victim of test anxiety, you're not alone, most people dread taking tests. For students, one of the most frequent stressful or anxiety-provoking experiences is taking tests. All students may feel some effects of the anxiety associated with tests. There are some people with text anxiety who are usually conscientious students who work hard and have high expectations of themselves. There are also some people who become very anxious at the thought of taking a test and they often convince themselves that they will fail.

WHEN SHOULD ONE OVERCOME ANXIETY?
You should practice these steps routinely. Don't wait until the day before the test to begin trying to overcome your anxiety. It is designed for those people who experience great trauma when they hear the word "test"! Try to find ways to step back from the cascade of worries before they swamp you.
From test anxiety to test frustration: The type of test anxiety can vary from being under-prepared for the test to the fear of failing the test, or anything in between. You may eventually get so tired and frustrated from this fear that you almost will not care anymore about doing well by the time the test date arrives! Make sure to take control of your anxiety before it crosses manageable levels.

DEGREE OF TEST ANXIETY:

Anxious feelings can range from a nervous feeling to forgetting and blanking-out to actually becoming physically ill. The nature and severity of test anxiety varies from one person to another. One individual may have mild anxiety but another may become incapacitated.

SEVERE ANXIETY: GET PROFESSIONAL HELP:

Everyone experiences some anxiety at some point in their life, which is normal. However, if you think that your anxiety is extreme or it continues to be a problem, or gets worse, it may be necessary to seek in-depth assistance from a trained professional counselor, therapist, or psychologist. These trained professionals can help you deal with the emotional components of test anxiety as well as introduce you to an array of techniques designed to give you control of the physical responses as well. Test anxiety is a serious issue and must be dealt with equal seriousness. It's not as simple as you stop worrying or thinking about your test, and it will dissipate automatically.

4.2: MYTHS ABOUT TEST ANXIETY:

MYTHS ABOUT TEST ANXIETY:
The most common misconception about test anxiety is that it is bad and you have to get rid of it. But the truth is that the objective of dealing with test anxiety should not be to completely get rid of it, but to understand it, bring it down to a manageable level, and hence feel more in control.

ACCEPTANCE – AVOIDANCE:
- **Acceptance:** Anxiety's worst enemy is acceptance, so the more you try to understand and get a perspective on your anxiety, the smaller it will get.
- **Avoidance:** Anxiety's best friend is avoidance/ignorance, so the more you try to avoid or ignore your anxiety, the bigger it will get.

MYTH #1: "If I feel anxious during a test, I have test anxiety."
This is a myth and it is not true.
Research shows everybody feels anxious during a test. This "anxiety" helps you to remain alert during the test. People who have test anxiety do not feel any more anxious or experience higher levels of physiological arousal than non-test anxious individuals. Test anxious individuals tend to concentrate on their anxiety or physiological arousal more than non-test anxious individuals.

MYTH #2: "If I experience test anxiety, I will do poorly on all my exams."
This is a myth and it is not true.
For the most part, this is not true. Research shows that test anxious individuals do not perform more poorly than non-test anxious individuals. The only time test anxious individuals may perform more poorly during tests is if they are spending most of their test-taking time concentrating on irrelevant information (worrying) instead of attending to the information on the test. Since full concentration on the test is necessary for peak performance, lower performance may occur. If the individual is able to change or stop competing thoughts during an exam, performance should not suffer.

MYTH #3: "I'm not as smart as other students if I experience test anxiety."
This is a myth and it is not true.
Actually, research shows that students with test anxiety tend to value academic success more than those who do not have test anxiety. They tend to work harder and in many cases get better grades than those without test anxiety. They interpret the grades, however, as lower than their non-test anxious peers.

4.3: TEST ANXIETY METER:

SOME TEST ANXIETY IS NATURAL AND COMMON:
There is no doubt about it, for most people, test-taking is stressful. Since test scores can determine whether you pass or fail a class, earn a scholarship, get admitted to a desired program, or even earn entry into a professional school, graduate program, job or career, it is natural to feel some anxiety when you take a test. In fact, it can be counter-productive not to have an awareness of the importance of the task at hand. Therefore, some anxiety is natural and it will help to keep you mentally and physically alert, but too much of anxiety may cause physical distress, emotional anguish, and concentration difficulties.

LITTLE TEST ANXIETY IS GOOD:
Some anxiety can be a powerful motivator. A certain degree of test anxiety is normal and may actually even work to your advantage. It will help motivate and prepare you more effectively for your test, study more efficiently, and take your test more carefully by remaining focused and alert. In fact, you can use your nervous energy to strengthen your performance on the test. It will help you focus and keep you on your toes. It's actually good to be concerned about taking your test, and being a little nervous is natural and may be inevitable while taking a test. Slight amount of anxiety frequently results in an improved test performance, but anxiety becomes a problem when it begins to adversely affect a person's performance on a test. It's not good when you have so much anxiety that you set yourself up for failure. Fear can be your worst enemy.

ZERO ANXIETY IS NOT GOOD:
Zero anxiety leads to ignorance. If you have no feelings of anxiety, you likely wouldn't care too much about the test and wouldn't spend the time needed to study for the test. An appropriate amount of anxiety primes you to prepare for a test; it will stimulate and sharpen your thinking. Always remember, it is better to have some anxiety and be well prepared for your examination than to have no anxiety and be unprepared.

EXCESSIVE TEST ANXIETY IS BAD:
Take the test seriously but don't blow its importance out of proportion. While some anxiety is normal and can even enhance one's performance, too much of it can actually hinder it and can reduce performance. Extreme test anxiety can transform into intense nervousness and that can negatively affect your performance. Some students experience test-related anxiety to such a degree that it interferes with their learning process and their ability to prepare for and perform on the tests to such an extent that it leads to poor performances. Excessive test anxiety can be detrimental and may prevent you from doing your real best on the test. In order to do your best, you cannot let test anxiety interfere in your performance, and cause a stumbling block in your pursuit of achieving whatever you are aiming for via your test.

DISADVANTAGES OF EXCESSIVE ANXIETY:
If you are suffering from test anxiety and are afraid of failures, you are more likely to become more anxious while taking a test and doubt your own abilities. High test anxiety blocks out what the students already know and significantly lowers their test performance. Anxiety can also stifle learning, or make the test preparation experience especially unpleasant. You will also be more likely to make mistakes which you might not otherwise. Ultimately, you will feel worked up and completely incompetent about the content of your test. Following are some of the disadvantages of excessive anxiety:
- **(A) Comprehension:** Having difficulty reading and understanding the questions on the test and taking more time than usual.
- **(B) Organization:** Having difficulty organizing your thoughts and being able to think with clarity.
- **(C) Recalling:** Having difficulty recalling previously learned material and going blank on some questions and then remembering the correct answers as soon as the test is over.
- **(D) Concentrating:** Having difficulty concentrating on the test and getting easily distracted without even any good reason.
- **(E) Planning:** Having difficulty in planning how to approach the test and how to implement the best techniques.
- **(F) Performance:** Having difficulty in being able to perform as well as you can and doing poorly on a test even though you know the material.

DO THE BALANCING ACT:
Since zero anxiety is counter productive and excessive anxiety can be detrimental, you must find the right balance, where your anxiety level is high enough to keep you on your toes and low enough not to come in your way. Why increase your anxiety and decrease your capacity to think, when you can balance it out?

4.4: REASONS FOR TEST ANXIETY:

WHY TEST ANXIETY OCCURS:

Some people suffer from test anxiety because, instead of feeling challenged by the prospects of success, they become more likely to be afraid of failure. They tend to become more pessimistic than optimistic. The pressure to perform well on tests can be a powerful motivator unless it is so extreme that it becomes irrational and more of a hindrance. Perfectionism and feelings of unworthiness provide unreasonable goals to achieve through testing situations. When a student's self-esteem is too closely tied up to the outcome of a single test, the results can be devastating. In this situation, students may spend more time focusing on the negative consequences of failure, instead of preparing for the test. Sometimes, test-anxiety is due to a negative test-taking experience, a negative attitude about school, low self-confidence, or a combination of all these. Usually, there is some real or perceived activating agent.

Test anxiety can be caused or developed due to a number of reasons, such as, lack of preparation in combination with the following factors:
- Poor time management.
- Poor study habits.
- Failure to organize text information.
- Lack of organization.
- Cramming the night before the test.

However, more complicated forms of test anxiety are also widespread. These forms tend to be more closely linked to one's personal feelings, experiences, and beliefs. Among these more complex forms, the most common causes typically fall into the following three categories:
- Feelings of helplessness.
- Fear of negative outcomes.
- Threats to self-worth.

FEELING OF HELPLESSNESS:

Feeling of helplessness leads to test fever, which is an acute form of nervousness that people who suffer from test anxiety experience before taking a test. The fear of a test is not an irrational or illegitimate fear, especially if how you perform on that test has the power to define or shape the course of your academic career and hence your future prospects in the advancement of your career and life. It's normal to connect a feeling of fear with an event. Excessive fear of a test can interfere with your ability to be successful in your career. There are many methods to treat test fever, some of which are discussed later in this section.

FEAR OF NEGATIVE OUTCOME:

Fear of failure or a negative outcome can very easily generate anxiety from many different sources in many different ways. Often, individuals become anxious before and during the test due to fear of failure. It is usually this type of thinking that leads to negative projections or fatalism that may immobilize a person or cause the person to "go blank" and not remember the information they have studied. You may have exaggerated the impact of an individual test, tying it directly to your career or life's success.

(A) **Fear of failure:** You may get worried that you will get a failing grade or a poor score and that will lead to projections of not completing a goal, i.e., passing the course, graduating from college, getting a job, etc. You may also believe that this test will jeopardize scholarships, financial aid, athletic eligibility, certification requirement, or insurance benefits.

(B) **Fear of embarrassment:** You might be concerned that you will embarrass yourself or your family by earning poor grades or low scores.

(C) **Fear of not being able to meet expectations:** You may be worried that you will not live up to the expectations of family and friends.

(D) **Negative Projections – Fatalism:** If an individual begins to think in a fatalistic way, it is most helpful to notice the negative expectation and counteract it with a positive expectation. Try to be sensitive to what you say to yourself.

THREATS TO SELF-WORTH:

Threats to self-worth and increased test anxiety can also result from putting too much emphasis on grades or scores. Some students insist on measuring their self-worth against the standards of A-B-C-D-E-F grades or the numerical scores. They tie their self-esteem too closely to their scores or grades, and in turn generate negative feelings about their abilities. These negative feelings erode their confidence and contribute to feelings of low self-esteem and self worth.

These feeling of failure, helplessness, and low self esteem will often manifest themselves in "negative self-talk". "Negative self-talk" is when students unknowingly increase their test anxiety by reinforcing negative beliefs about themselves and their circumstances.

ANXIETY SELF TEST:

While taking a test, when suddenly your mind goes blank, your heart races, your palms sweat, and your stomach flip-flops, you are experiencing more than ordinary test-jitters. Psychologists define this extreme reaction as "test anxiety." If not checked properly on time, it can undermine your performance any time you're on the hot seat.

One of the quickest and easiest ways to determine whether you have symptoms of an anxiety disorder is by taking an anxiety self test. Self tests or screening tests are developed to help you recognize the signs of an anxiety disorder. They are not intended to provide a conclusive diagnosis or replace a proper evaluation by a professional counselor. Regardless of the results, contact your professional counselor if you have any serious concerns.

WHILE TAKING A TEST, DO YOU EXPERIENCE ANY OF THE FOLLOWING?

- Feel like you are going completely "blank"?
- Find the words meaningless while reading test questions?
- Do you need to reread test questions several times in order to comprehend them?
- Score much lower than on practice exercises or practice tests?
- Become frustrated?
- Feel like the room is closing in on you?
- Feel your heart racing or find it difficult to breathe?
- Become distracted?
- Feel overwhelmed?
- Have distracting thoughts of failure or a poor performance?
- Forget what you are supposed to do?
- Suddenly "know" the answers after turning in the test?

If you answer "yes" to some of the above questions, you may be experiencing test and/or performance anxiety.

4.5: TYPES OF TEST ANXIETY:

(A) TYPES OF ANXIETIES BASED ON RATIONALITY:

(I) RATIONAL ANXIETY:

Rational anxiety is the anxiety that is a direct result of lack of preparation and knowledge about the test. Under-preparation and/or lack of knowledge can cause high levels of stress and anxiety. This type of test anxiety is quite common, and fortunately it can be easily alleviated by properly studying and preparing for your test.

DIFFERENCE BETWEEN TEST ANXIETY & LACK OF PREPARATION:

Is it really anxiety or just lack of preparation? Students often blame test anxiety for poor performance on tests. However, this poor performance on the tests may be a result of lack of preparedness for a test (which also causes anxiety), instead of classic test anxiety. Be sure to know the difference between the two and be well prepared. If several symptoms of test anxiety are present, you may be experiencing the real test anxiety.

Feelings of helplessness can emerge when students miss the connection between their own behavior and their test's outcome. Instead of blaming their poor performance on their own lack of preparation, they blame their performances on the difficulty of the test, the inadequacy of the instructor, or other circumstances outside their control. This external focus of blame leaves them feeling victimized, helpless, out of control, and anxious. As a result, they waste valuable time contemplating their own predicament and then they don't study because they are convinced that nothing can help.

(I) IRRATIONAL ANXIETY:

Irrational anxiety is the anxiety that occurs when you are adequately prepared for your test but you still feel the stress or nervousness associated with taking a test.

Both these types of anxieties are considered quite normal, anyone can have them, and there are many ways to overcome their effect.

(B) TYPES OF ANXIETIES BASED ON LOCATION AND TIME:

(i) **Performance Anxiety:** Anxiety can be labeled as "performance anxiety" if it occurs while performing challenging or critical functions, such as a test.

(i) **Anticipatory Anxiety:** Anxiety can be labeled as "anticipatory anxiety" if you experience a feeling of agitation and distress while studying and thinking about what might happen when you take a test. If you have any prior negative experience with test-taking, it can serve as an activating agent. For students who have a fear of performing well in testing situations, it can develop into anticipatory anxiety. Worrying about how anxiety will influence you can be as incapacitating as the anxiety itself. This kind of anxiety can build as the testing situation approaches, and can interfere with the student's ability to prepare adequately and perform satisfactorily.

(iii) **Situational Anxiety:** Anxiety can be labeled as "situational anxiety" if it occurs in specific situations, such as while taking a test.

(iv) **Occasional Anxiety:** Anxiety can be labeled as "occasional anxiety" if it occurs only occasionally due to some external factors.

(v) **Waiting Anxiety:** Anxiety can be labeled as "waiting anxiety" if it occurs while waiting for the event to occur, such as, while waiting for the test. If waiting for the test to begin causes anxiety, distract yourself by self talking and reinforcing some positive thoughts discussed later in this chapter. You have waited for this moment for a long time – a few more minutes should not matter.

4.6: COMPONENTS OF TEST ANXIETY:

COMPONENTS OF TEST ANXIETY:
Test anxiety can be broken down into the following four different, but related components:

(A) PHYSIOLOGICAL COMPONENT:
The physiological component of test anxiety involves the typical bodily reactions that you experience before, during, and after the test due to acute test anxiety when your body physically responds to stress and anxiety.

PHYSIOLOGICAL SIGNS OF TEST ANXIETY:
- Excessive perspiration/sweating – like sweaty palms or underarms.
- Dry mouth or extreme thirst.
- Shaking or trembling hands.
- Headaches.
- Pounding heartbeat or rapid pulse.
- Shortness of breath – difficulty breathing properly.
- Stomachaches – feel like there is a knot in the stomach.
- Nausea – feeling of butterflies in the stomach.
- Fainting/dizziness or lightheadedness.
- Tense muscles – ache in the shoulders, back of the neck, etc.
- Extreme body temperature changes – suddenly feeling cold to hot and vice versa.
- Insomnia – lack of sleep, tiredness, fatigue, etc.
- Appetite change – extreme and sudden increase or decrease in appetite.

(B) EMOTIONAL COMPONENT:
The emotional/psychological component of test anxiety involves the typical emotional reactions or feelings that you experience before, during, and after the test due to acute test anxiety when you respond to stress and anxiety emotionally.

EMOTIONAL SIGNS OF TEST ANXIETY:
- Panic attacks.
- Excessive feelings and fear of failure – being afraid of the negative consequences of failure.
- Disappointment.
- Anger.
- Depression.
- Feelings of apprehension.
- Frustration.
- Embarrassment.
- Uncontrollable crying or laughing – continuously crying or laughing without being able to stop.
- Feelings of helplessness.
- Guilt.
- Boredom.
- Self-doubt.

(C) MENTAL/COGNITIVE COMPONENT:
The mental or cognitive component of test anxiety involves the typical thoughts that run through your mind before, during, and after the test due to acute anxiety when you respond to stress and anxiety mentally.

MENTAL SIGNS OF TEST ANXIETY:
- Mental Block – temporary "freeze up" or "going blank" – like going blank on a question and remembering it as soon as the test is over.
- Lack of confidence.
- Lack of Attention – difficulty concentrating – being easily distracted during the test.
- Difficulty reading/comprehending test questions.

- Disorientation – difficulty organizing your thoughts.
- Confusion – racing thoughts with no clarity.
- Inability to make decisions – not being able to decide which one is the correct/best answer.
- Inability to express yourself.
- Excessive worry – worry about the future, about doing well, about success, about your performance compared to others.
- Forgetfulness or loss of memory – trouble recalling/retrieving information that you previously learned and which you actually know.
- Past test memories – previous failures on the test.
- Negative self-talk or thoughts.
- Being extremely self critical.

(D) BEHAVIORAL COMPONENT:
The behavioral component of test anxiety involves the typical bodily reactions that you experience before, during, and after the test due to acute anxiety when your body responds to stress and anxiety behaviorally.

BEHAVIORAL SIGNS OF TEST ANXIETY:
- Fidgeting – like tapping your fingers on the desk.
- Pacing – like walking back and forth quickly.
- Substance abuse – like taking excessive alcohol or drugs.
- Avoidance – like plotting ways to escape from the test by sneaking out, faking an illness, etc.
- Procrastination – like avoiding the task at hand and doing something else.

THIS PAGE HAS BEEN INTENTIONALLY LEFT BLANK.

PART 5.0: ANXIETY MANAGEMENT:

TABLE OF CONTENTS:

THIS PAGE HAS BEEN INTENTIONALLY LEFT BLANK.

5.1: PSYCHE YOURSELF:

TEST ANXIETY IS MANAGEABLE AND CURABLE:

Test anxiety is common, understandable, manageable, and curable. Overcoming test anxiety isn't easy. It takes work and concentration, practice and more practice. But if you are determined to succeed and you are willing to take the necessary steps, you will be able to take a test and feel confident that you know what you are doing. Fortunately, test anxiety can be dealt with and brought under control by taking some measures. There is a great deal that you can do to keep the anxiety from interfering with your performance. First, it's important to know that you don't have to eliminate it entirely. It helps to be "up" for exams. You just have to reduce the anxiety to a manageable level. In some cases, test anxiety can be reduced or eliminated by working on test-taking skills, such as strategies for answering different types of questions, and then hone them through practice questions.

UNDERSTAND YOUR ANXIETY:

To treat any problem, you have to first understand what the problem is, what caused the problem, where it was generated from, and so forth. The more you are able to understand the cycle of behaviors, thoughts, emotions, and feelings involved in your test related anxiety, the easier you will be able to intervene and do something more adaptive and conducive in order to lower your anxiety level. So first, try to identify and describe your inner thoughts that are causing the anxiety. Focus your attention on your anxiety and think about the feelings it generates. If you can completely experience a physical sensation, it will often disappear.

TEST ANXIETY IS A LEARNED TRAIT WHICH CAN BE UNLEARNED:

Since test anxiety is learned behavior, it can be unlearned. The first step is to determine where or why this behavior began and then begin the process of unlearning or reversing the response.

MAP OUT YOUR ANXIETY CYCLE:

Map out your anxiety cycle including thoughts, behaviors, physiological responses and emotions and when they occur in the sequence.
- When the fear kicks in, just pause.
- Keep the focus on the present task.
- Don't try to eliminate fear totally; just reduce it to a manageable level.
- You are a logical thinker; you can reason your fear away.
- You can convince yourself to do it.
- Do something that will prevent you from thinking about fear.
- Just take one step at a time.

TEST ANXIETY MANAGEMENT CAN BE A SLOW PROCESS:

Test anxiety takes time to develop and to go away. Whatever may be the degree or level of your anxiety, fortunately research has shown that there are several things that can be done to alleviate your stress and anxiety and make test anxiety more manageable. Be patient with yourself and keep trying to figure out ways that reduce your stress level by applying all the strategies mentioned in this book.

POSTPONE YOUR ANXIETY UNTIL AFTER THE TEST:

Postpone the anxiety by telling yourself that you will have enough time to get anxious later. Now is the time to take the test, not to worry about the consequences! While taking the test, don't waste your time worrying about the consequences of not doing well on the test. So clear your mind of any anxious thoughts or worries that may linger. First try to do your best on the test, and then you will have enough time to think or worry about your result.

DON'T GLOBALIZE NEGATIVE OUTCOME:

People with test anxiety tend to "catastrophize." This means that they see the probable or likely outcome of an event to be far more negative and global than it really is. In addition, many students also have "black and white thinking." This means that they view test performance as "perfect success" or "failure."

WAYS TO REDUCE RATIONAL ANXIETY:

Your best defense is a good offense, so be well prepared for the test. Preparation is the best way to minimize rationale anxiety.

- It may all begin with insufficient performance on a particular test, which then creates a general fear of the testing situation that hampers future performance, creating a vicious cyclical reaction of anxiety and low scores.
- Last minute cramming will lead to feeling less confident about the material covered than those who have been able to follow a structured plan for studying. If you already know what to expect and know that material well, it'll help you take the test with a more positive attitude.

Preparation/Skills/Knowledge: The best strategy to control test anxiety is to be thoroughly prepared prior to the test. Getting well prepared for the test is more than half the battle won. Nothing will give you more confidence than knowing that you are adequately prepared for the test. Getting effective preparation is the key to test success. Remember that it is better to have a little anxiety and be well prepared than to have no test anxiety and no preparation. Realizing in the midst of a test that you are not well prepared can throw you into a panic mode.

You should master all the test preparation skills given all throughout this book, some of them are listed below:

- Develop effective study and test preparation skills.
- Follow the seven step study plan.
- Review and re-review material.
- Over-study for the test.
- Learn test-taking strategies.
- Spread review over several days rather than cramming.
- Practice time/stress Management.
- Integrate ideas from review material, strategies, notes, and any other supplemental aid.

WAYS TO REDUCE IRRATIONAL ANXIETY:

Inward-Outward: The various physical and emotional symptoms of test anxiety have the common effect of focusing your attention and energy inward on your immediate, personal feelings and circumstance as opposed to focusing on the task at hand. Many of the strategies available to combat test anxiety encourage you to focus your energies outward on test preparation and performance.

5.2: ANXIETY CONTROL PROCEDURE:

If you feel overly anxious, this process will help you attain a relaxed, calm, tranquil, and restful state, and will also produce more energy available for remembering, thinking, and writing. You will begin feeling more relaxed, calm and tranquil, and because you have been focusing on this exercise, you will forget about your anxiety. When you are relaxed, you'll have all of your energy focused on your work with none wasted in worrying. Stay calm, and loosen up to regain your composure.

RELAXATION TECHNIQUES:

Relaxation techniques are the best way to reduce test anxiety. When used with mental and physical preparation, relaxation before and during a test can aid retention and significantly improve test performance. Relaxation will help reduce tension, release any anxiety that you may have, and help clear your mind for study and review.

There are three basic relaxation techniques that are an effective way to lower your level of stress/tension. All these techniques can be used in any test related stressful situation as it's not visible and pretty silent. You should first practice each one of them individually and then combine all three of them so that you can use them simultaneously for more effective relaxation. You should experience complete relaxation, not just partial relaxation.

Learning how to relax Is fairly simple, but if you want to be able to use it on your next test, you will have to practice it beforehand. The relaxation techniques require some practice, so make sure you practice them enough for more effectiveness.

WHEN TO APPLY RELAXATION TECHNIQUES:

Whenever you realize you are feeling anxious while studying, reviewing, waiting for the test to begin, or actually taking the test, begin using these techniques, especially if concentration is wandering or energy is waning. In short, practice relaxing techniques so that it becomes an automatically learned response. The more you practice them, the better it will work.

DO THE FOLLOWING BEFORE PRACTICING ANY RELAXATION TECHNIQUES:

- Close your test booklet – place your answer sheet and pencil in the middle of the test booklet.
- Let your mind go blank – take a moment away from the questions, shut out all your thoughts.
- Get comfortable in your chair – sit down in the most relaxed position that you can – rest your arms on the side, slouch down if that helps.
- Close your eyes – calm yourself down, and let your mind and body relax.

APPLY THE FOLLOWING TECHNIQUES TO COMPOSE AND RELAX YOURSELF, AND RELIEVE ANXIETY:

(A) MUSCLE RELAXATION:

When it's time to take the test, pay attention to the muscles in your arms, shoulders and jaws. If they're tight, it's because you're a little uptight and tense. Just like a tense mind can tighten up your muscles, relaxing your muscles can loosen you up mentally.

EZ-STEP-BY-STEP METHOD: Apply the following steps to do muscle relaxation.

STEP 1: Tighten: Contract tense muscles in each part of your body that you're clenching, (jaw, neck, stomach) starting from your head and then move down towards your toe.

STEP 2: Stretch: Bend and rotate your head from side to side around your shoulders in all directions, turning your head and eyes to look as far back over each shoulder as you can.
- **(i)** First, bend your head forward and try to bend down your chin as close as you can to your chest.
- **(ii)** Next, bend your head backward and try to bend down your head as close as you can to your back.
- **(iii)** Next, bend your left ear as close as you can to your left shoulder.
- **(iv)** Finally, bend your right ear as close as you can to your right shoulder.

STEP 3: Relax: Take a deep breath and count to five. Assume normal position, relax and exhale.

NOTE THE FOLLOWING:

- Repeat the above process (tighten-stretch-relax) throughout the test whenever you feel anxious.

- This whole procedure should take only about a minute.
- Concentrate on making each muscle relax more and more completely.
- Repeat the process with the muscles of your face and jaw, neck, shoulders, arms, chest, etc., until you reach your toes.
- Feel the muscles stretch on one side of your neck as they contract on the other.

(B) CONTROLLED BREATHING:

Most of us breathe improperly or erratically most of the time by taking shallow breaths. We breathe using only the upper part of our chest and shoulder muscles. We tend to take quick breaths and never get quite enough oxygen into our bodies. When an insufficient amount of fresh air reaches our lungs, our blood is not properly purified or oxygenated. Poorly oxygenated blood contributes to anxiety states, depression, and fatigue, and makes each stressful situation many times harder to cope with. Proper breathing habits are essential for good mental and physical health. Improper breathing hurts confidence and it interferes with clear thinking. Hence, in order to get a better grip on the test, breathe deeply in a slow, relaxed manner.

INHALE-HOLD-EXHALE TECHNIQUE:

EZ-STEP-BY-STEP METHOD: Apply the following steps to do controlled breathing:

STEP 1: Inhale: Breathe-in slowly and deeply through your nose to the count of seven – fill your lungs and abdomen – imagine yourself smelling your favorite fragrance– say "peace" to yourself.

STEP 2: Hold Your Breath: After inhaling and before exhaling, hold your breath to the count of seven.

STEP 3: Exhale: Breath-out slowly and easily through your mouth to the count of seven – empty your lungs and abdomen – imagine yourself blowing a candle – say "relax" to yourself.

NOTE THE FOLLOWING:

- Repeat the above process (inhale-hold-exhale) throughout the test whenever you feel anxious.
- This whole procedure should take only about a minute.
- When you feel relaxed and ready, open your eyes, open your test booklet, and get back to work.
- Compare your present relaxed state of mind with your previous tense feelings, and you'll see the difference.
- As you exhale, concentrate on pushing all of the tension out of your lungs.
- Focus your attention and concentrate on your rhythmic in-and-out flow of breath going in and out through your airways, and don't think of anything else.
- Don't breathe too fast or forcefully because this may cause hyperventilation.

(C) VISUALIZATION:

Lowering your autonomic arousal may make it less intrusive and less aversive during tests. You can do this by slowing down your breathing through deep breaths or closing your eyes and thinking of something pleasurable. Visualizing has the added advantage of changing what you are thinking about during a test which may help change your negative thoughts to more positive ones.

GUIDED IMAGERY AND VISUALIZATION: PEACEFUL SCENE TECHNIQUE:

EZ-STEP-BY-STEP METHOD: Apply the following steps to do visualization.

STEP 1: Imagine: Visualize and imagine yourself in your favorite place in a peaceful, pleasant, natural, beautiful, and soothing scene, such as a beach or a mountain – somewhere you have been before, somewhere quiet where you feel calm and relaxed.

STEP 2: Concentrate: Concentrate on the scene and try to clearly visualize the picture, and imagine yourself actually present on the scene.

STEP 3: Feel: To make the effects of the scene feel more real, try to experience the total scene as well as the associated sensations, try to imagine what you see, feel, hear, and smell – such as, the sound of the ocean, crying of the seagulls, sand running through your fingers, sun on your skin, blue sky, the taste of salt water, the smell and saltiness in the wind.

NOTE THE FOLLOWING:

- Keep the relaxed scene in your mind for a few minutes.

- If you still feel anxious, stop, imagine something else, and try to relax again.

VISUALIZATION – POSITIVE TEST REHEARSAL:

Visualize taking the test successfully – rehearse taking your test weeks before the actual test date. Play the entire "tape" in your mind – what is going to happen on test day, from the moment you wake up on the day of the test to the moment you finish the test. Imagine yourself getting up in the morning, following your morning routine, and then going off to take the test.

We mostly tend to live up to our own expectations, good or bad. If you spend a lot of time mentally rehearsing what you will do when you fail, you increase your chances of failure. So take time to rehearse what it will be like to succeed – be specific and imagine it in considerable detail, and in a totally positive way. Visualization really works; even professional athletes and actors regularly use this technique to improve their performances. If you can visualize something, you can make it happen too!

Before your exam, practice imagining yourself as capable and confident and view the exam as an opportunity to show what you know. You may want to practice the following typical sequence to visualize taking the test successfully.

TYPICAL SEQUENCE:

Imagine the following typical sequence:
- Imagine yourself getting up in the morning, and having some breakfast.
- Next, visualize yourself driving to the test center and walking into the test room, sitting down, and getting ready to take the test.
- Next, hear the other students shuffle in their seats.
- Next, feel the desk, the pencil in your hand and see the test in front of you.
- Next, visualize yourself looking over the test calmly and confidently.
- Next, visualize yourself discovering that the questions are perfectly clear to you and you know all the answers.
- Next, visualize yourself working on the questions – quickly, confidently, and accurately.
- Next, visualize completing the test successfully.
- Next, when you have finished, hand in your test and walk self-confidently out of the room, experiencing the feeling of having done well.
- Next, breathe a sigh of relief and satisfaction.
- Next, imagine it is several days later.
- Next, you receive the results of your test.
- Next, you look at the test score with confidence, and you see an excellent score – better than what you anticipated.
- Next, you congratulate yourself and give the news to your family and friends.
- Next, you celebrate your success with your friends.
- Finally, when you feel completely relaxed, let your thoughts return to reality.

Rehearse this scenario a number of times before the actual test.

FOCUSING ON PAST SUCCESS:

Think of a real-life situation in which you did well on a test or any other major project and then focus on this success. Next, bring yourself back to the test while still keeping your thoughts and feelings about that successful experience at the back of your head. Don't over analyze or try to make comparisons between the two events. Simply imagine yourself taking the test with the same level of confidence and optimism.

GIVING TEST REHEARSAL A MORE PRACTICAL APPROACH:

Imagine yourself taking a test in a real test like situation. Sit in a classroom similar to where the actual test will be given and imagine you are taking it. Practice taking several timed practice or mock tests.

Desensitization: Another aspect of rehearsal is desensitization. It will make you less responsive to an overwhelming fear by repeated exposure to the feared situation or object, either in natural or artificial circumstances. By repeatedly putting yourself in the testing position and experiencing a comfortable feeling, you will be desensitizing yourself to those bad feelings. This means you need to take as much of the "scare" out of the test as possible. If you can, visit the actual site of the test and walk around the room – anything you can do to desensitize yourself to the testing environment.

5.3: TAKE CONTROL OF THE TEST:

GREAT "TEST" EXPECTATIONS:

You must have test expectations that are realistic. Your beliefs about something create expectations about how a situation will play out. Set your belief system and expectations so that they are realistically achievable and attainable. Remember that the most reasonable expectation is to at least be able to demonstrate as much of what you know as you possibly can.

IF YOU BELIEVE IT, YOU CAN DO IT:

You have to first believe in yourself that you are actually capable of performing well on the test and that you will be able to get your desired score. Your belief about something generates expectations and that in turn leads to a stronger determination in making those expectations or goals transform into reality. Stay away from negative beliefs, since they normally generate negative expectations of failure. If you say negative things to yourself about your abilities, it produces a corresponding negative emotional reaction and anxiety. Negative expectations then create anxiety and this anxiety will disable you from actually doing well. Anxiety is created by expectations or thoughts about what is likely to happen.

For example, if you believe you are not intelligent, don't know the information well enough, or are not capable of performing well on tests, then your expectations will be of a failure. It is impossible to achieve something that you don't even believe in. Therefore, first believe in yourself and your abilities, and thus have positive expectations for how you will perform on the test, and negate any negative feelings. Soon, you will realize that you have already won half the battle of test-taking by keeping up your spirits and a positive belief system, and you will be much more likely to perform better on your next test.

TEMPORARY AMNESIA:

Working under pressure can sometimes lead to temporary amnesia. It is a fairly common thing for students to forget previously learned information while under pressure. After studying very hard, as soon as they start taking the test, their minds go completely blank. Most of the information that they knew very well suddenly dissipates or vanishes as they get on that hot seat. It's not that they are inadequately prepared for the test or are not intelligent or capable enough to perform well on the test, it is obviously something else. It is clear that these students are going through some serious problem, the problem of being able to recall previously learned information when the time of testing their knowledge comes. Much of this is attributable to the conflict between their "imagination" and their "will". Whenever the imagination and will are in conflict, the imagination always wins out. The will of the student is to do well on the test. The student studies very hard and knows the information backward and forward. Then the big moment comes and fear takes over his/her imagination. All the horrible thoughts start to inhabit and dominate the imagination. Finally, the imagination wins out by creating temporary "amnesia" for the information needed to perform well on the test. If the student doesn't fail the test, he/she certainly will achieve a test score much lower than they deserve. Now this is a serious problem and it must be dealt with equal seriousness. You need to eliminate all the fear and the negative thoughts out of your mind and transform them into more positive thoughts. The first step in achieving something is to first believe in it and have enough confidence in yourself that you can achieve it.

FEAR OF UNKNOWN:

Most of the test-fear that people have when taking a test is fear of the unknown. You can fight these fears with a few ideas on how to get better prepared.

(A) Test Format: You should also be familiar with all the aspects of the test format and study accordingly. Find out in advance as much information as you possibly can about the test format so that you know what to expect and there will be no surprises.

(B) Test Content: The most important aspect of getting ready for a test is to master all the material.

(C) Test-Taking Skills: The second most important part is to learn test-taking skills and how to use them effectively.

FEAR OF SUBJECT:

Fear of subject is one of the biggest causes of not being able to perform better on the tests. Some students have a preconceived notion that a particular subject is extremely hard. Since childhood, they have been told this by their teacher. You must eliminate any sort of fear from your mind and think that it's not rocket science. If others can do well, so can you. If you have a fear in your mind, you will not be able to learn and understand what you study. Just imagine that you are driving a car with your mind full of fear; you will be more likely to get into an accident. Likewise, if you are studying for a test with a lot of fear in your mind, you are more likely to make mistakes. Students, who say that math is the most dreadful subject, say that because they have never actually tried to understand it or no one has ever been able to make them understand it. Once they study with a free mind, they realize that it's just like any other subject. Fear is a mental disease and the only way to treat it is by giving the subject a fair chance to try to understand it before categorizing it as "difficult" or "dreadful". Everyone deserves a fair chance before a verdict, and so does every subject.

DEVELOPING GOOD MENTAL CONDITIONING:

It is obviously important to be thoroughly familiar with the principle and content covered in our content-based books. It is equally important to be equipped with the strategies and techniques you'll need to tackle different question types covered in our strategy books. But in order to put all your preparation to work in the most effective manner, there is one important thing which you must not ignore. And, that one important component is being able to take control of your test by developing the right attitude and mindset which will help you tremendously in your preparation and your success on the test. Of course, just having the right attitude or confidence by itself isn't enough to ensure good performance on your test, but a lack of confidence can seriously damage your performance. Once you are armed with the weapons (content and strategies) that you need to do well on the test, you must learn how to exploit those armaments with the right frame of mind, in the right spirit, and in the right way. You have nothing to worry about, we have it all covered in this book. Once you understand and follow the approach explained in this book, you'll develop the right attitude and feel more confident and perform your best by putting your knowledge to its best use.

YOU CONTROL YOUR MIND AND SOUL:

Your brain believes what you want it to believe, your mind learns what you want it to learn, and your heart feels what you want it to feel – so always keep a positive attitude by telling yourself that you will do well and that you are well prepared for the test. Make a list of the things you can do and want to achieve, the things you want to think and the feelings you want to feel – all this will contribute to a positive mental attitude. Challenge yourself to do the best you can. Do not give up before your game has even started!

BE IN CONTROL:

You can't control the testing situation or the test itself, but you can definitely learn how to control yourself. If you don't have a sense of control, it can easily lead to stress and anxiety, and you may begin to feel helpless and hopeless. Be in control and put yourself in charge while taking the test. Simply follow the steps listed in this section, don't let anything or anyone bother you or get to you. Remember, if you are in control of yourself, you will be optimizing your performance on the test and improving the chances of getting a score you deserve. So just sit back, relax, and take the test! This is the best way to make sure that you do your best on the test.

Develop a sense for your role in your outcomes. Resist the temptation to blame your circumstances and outcomes on situations and people you can't control. It is important to recognize your own contributions and to focus on what you can control - your own behavior. A belief that you can control your outcomes will motivate you to work harder, lead to greater rewards, and in turn will reinforce your sense of control.

PUT THE TEST IN PERSPECTIVE:

We realize that it's very important for you to do well on your test, but you must put the test in perspective. Try not to give your test a "larger than life" persona. View the test as simply "another test," when you exaggerate or inflate the importance of a particular test, you unnecessarily increase your test anxiety. After all, a test is only a test; in fact, it is just one test in a series of tests you are going to be taking during your lifetime. Your performance on one test is not that big of a deal. If you don't pass it or get a good score this time, you can always take it again. Contrary to popular belief, no one test can single-handedly determine the outcome of your entire academic career. Remember, it's you taking the test, not the test-taking you.

SEE YOUR TEST AS A CHALLENGE, NOT A THREAT:

Analyze each reason very rationally and objectively. Think about the worst that could possibly happen to you if you don't get a good score. By spending some time analyzing each cause of your concern, you will come to realize that in fact, there is nothing that can damage you permanently if you do happen to get a bad score. Lots of students get bad scores but it does not mean they give up. Many of them return with a vengeance and perform much better – they are the strugglers and survivors in life. They make a new plan when the chips are down. Therefore, try to see an exam as a **challenge** rather than a **threat** so that your negative attitude turns into a positive one and helps you feel more motivated and less anxious.

DON'T GIVE A TEST THE POWER TO DEFINE YOU:

Don't give a test the power to define you. A test cannot determine whether you are brilliant or not. Your performance on a test mostly depends on how well you studied for the test, the quality of your prior education, and the test-taking strategies you use.

There is no doubt about it, for most people, tests are stressful. Because test scores can determine whether you pass or fail a class, earn a scholarship, get admitted to desired program, or even earn entry into a professional school, graduate program, job or career, it is natural to feel some anxiety when you take a test. In fact, it can be counter-productive not to have an awareness of the importance of the task at hand.

TESTS MAY NOT BE A TRUE INDICATOR OF ONE'S ABILITY: DON'T CONNECT TEST SCORES WITH SELF-WORTH:

Tests are used to measure a student's knowledge and skills. Sometimes, the results of a test may or may not give a clear picture of the student's knowledge because of test anxiety. An individual may do poorly on a test but know the material. The person's poor performance is largely due to anxiety. In general, people are not comfortable taking tests. However, the feeling of apprehension or challenge often causes us not to give our best effort. Moreover, one can't judge anyone's skills or abilities on the basis of a single test score. Test scores are not perfect measures of what a person can or cannot do. There are many other variables that play a role or might influence the final outcome in this equation, which in this case is the test score. Remember that your test score is not a measure of self-worth. For some people, decoupling this connection can be hard to do. A test only measures your performance on a given day. It tells you how much you know about the questions you were asked. It is not a measure of your worth as a student. It is important that you see the test in this manner and not let your score become a reflection of you. For example, a person's test score can be affected by the way he or she is feeling, mood, attitude, alertness, the setting in the classroom, etc.

However, tests do reflect a person's overall achievement. The more effort and energy a person puts into learning, the more likely he/she will perform well on tests. Practicing test-taking and test anxiety management techniques can help you to be prepared, overcome test anxiety, and portray a clearer picture of your actual knowledge and skills. Also remember that one test is simply one test.

DON'T MAKE YOUR TEST A LIFE AND DEATH PROPOSITION:

Don't overplay the importance of a test – it is not a reflection of your self-worth nor does it predict your future success. So don't treat the test as a chance of a lifetime and don't make it a life and death proposition. One test is only a small part of the long process of your education and training. A little disappointment, inconvenience, and somewhat wounded ego are normal. So don't let the test get onto you, instead you should get onto your test!

DON'T MAGNIFY THE IMPORTANCE OF A TEST:

Interestingly, many students report that their initial thoughts are the ones of worries, regarding their performance on the test, but these thoughts quickly spiral into worries about the test reflecting their worth as a person. In other words, the test is no more just about what was learned in school, but it is a reflection of the individual's worth and ability.

IMPROVE YOUR PERSPECTIVE ON THE TEST:

Improving your perspective of the whole test-taking experience can actually help you enjoy studying or preparing for the test and it can even improve your performance on the test. Approach the test vigorously and be determined that you will do your best; but also accept the limits of what you know at the moment. Use everything you know to do well; but don't blame yourself for what you don't know.

CONSEQUENCES OF YOUR TEST SCORE:

Changing how you interpret the consequences of your performance on tests may help eliminate some of the worries involved in test anxiety. Failure on one question or one section or even one test will not ruin your life. Look at things more realistically. Think of the number of tests you take over your entire academic or professional career, about 120 or more. Doing poorly on a few of them will not have too much of an effect on your life.

ALL YOU CAN DO IS YOUR BEST: DON'T BE TOO HARD ON YOURSELF:

When you take a test, you are simply demonstrating your ability to think analytically or to understand what you learned in school or to perhaps perform certain tasks. It has been demonstrated time and again that whenever you carry an extra emotional baggage, performance suffers. There is no more effective manner to overdose yourself on anxiety than to lose perspective of the big picture. The best way to optimize your performance is to focus on the task at hand, devoid

of extraneous pressures, and strive to do the best you can at that point in time, not the best you "should" or "would like to do" or "could have done".
You're mantra should be:
- "I simply want to do the best I am capable of right now."
- "The most I can do is my best."
- "Be the best I can be."

That's all you have control over, and this is all you should focus upon.

YOU SHOULD REALIZE THE FOLLOWING FACTS AND PUT THE TEST IN PERSPECTIVE:

- The test is only one of the factors in your school/college admission decision making process.
- Your school grades are considered to be a very important criterion while making an admission decision by most admission officers.
- There are other nonacademic factors which are considered to be important criteria while making an admission decision. These include, letter of recommendation, extra curricular activities, etc. Working hard across these elements may make the performance on an individual test less critical and a smaller piece of a greater plan.
- Your essays also play a very important role in your application for admission.
- Your personal interview can also make an effect on the admission decision.

Note: Different schools/colleges pay different weight to the factors listed above.

PUT YOUR ROLE AS A STUDENT IN PERSPECTIVE:

We often see ourselves as students and then define our status as a student by our test scores. It is important to think more broadly about who we are. Prompt yourself to think about your other roles. Being a student is only one facet or dimension of our multi faceted or dimensional life. You are sons or daughters, fathers or mothers, brothers or sisters, friends, employees, volunteers, partners, artists, athletes, musicians, cooks, and multitudes of other things. Put your role as a student in perspective and then work to maximize your performance in that area.

Bottom Line: Last but not the least, even if you don't do as well as you expected to on the test, it is not the end of the world; you can always take the test again. Remember, when you don't get what you want, you get experience, and make that experience work in your favor when you take the test again next time. So don't lose your hopes and keep fighting with the right spirit and you will succeed one day. Try, try, and try again – keep trying until you succeed.

5.4: THE RIGHT ATTITUDE:

THE RIGHT POSITIVE ATTITUDE:

It may sound a bit strange but your attitude towards the test can significantly affect your performance. Having the right positive mental attitude is a time proven attribute for success on the test.

The following are a few things you can implement to make sure you develop the right positive attitude for the test:
- Look at the test as an opportunity to show off your skills and that you can match your intellect with that of the test makers, not as an instrument of punishment.
- Look at the test as a challenge but not as an obsession; keep a balance where you feel challenged enough but don't blow it out of proportion by obsessing over it.

The following are some facts about having the right positive attitude for the test:
- Those people who approach the test as an obstruction or a necessity of taking the test usually don't perform as well as those who see the test as an opportunity to showcase their ability to think analytically and reason logically.
- Those people who approach the test as a means to show the world what they are capable of and how they are different from the rest are likely to perform better than those who resent or dread it.

Finally, remember that you're more prepared for the test than most people. You've made use of the EZ Solutions set of books. You are armed with everything you need – the content, the strategies, and the skills of how to most effectively put your knowledge to the best use.

ATTITUDE, MOOD & THOUGHTS:

Your attitude and mood play a very important role while you are taking the test. The attitude you bring with you to a test has a lot to do with how you perform on the test. You may be very well prepared for the test and know all the material completely, but if you are in a bad mood, depressed, feeling down, or not feeling good, it can adversely affect your performance on the test. Think positive and tell yourself that you can do this. Don't let any negative thoughts enter your mind while taking the test. Any sort of negativity can adversely affect your performance on the test. Therefore, keep a positive attitude and be confident while taking the test.

Your attitude should be to:
- encourage yourself.
- develop reasonable and realistic expectations.
- think of the test as an opportunity to demonstrate your capabilities and abilities.
- realize that the test is only one measure of your overall ability.
- emphasize that test scores do not determine your worth.
- test scores may not necessarily reflect your true abilities.
- not over emphasize the importance of the test.

POSITIVE THOUGHTS GENERATE CONFIDENCE & NEGATIVE THOUGHTS GENERATE ANXIETY:

Anxiety is primarily created by the expectation or thoughts about what is likely to happen.

Positive Attitude: If you have a positive attitude about your abilities – it will produce a corresponding positive emotional reaction, which leads to positive performance.

Negative Attitude: If you have a negative attitude about your abilities – it will produce a corresponding negative emotional reaction, which leads to negative performance.

TRANSFORM NEGATIVE THOUGHTS INTO POSITIVE THOUGHTS:

Reverse and replace the negative thoughts and turn them into positive thoughts. Learn to recognize negative thoughts and quickly contradict and combat them with positive and self-supportive statements. One of the major causes of test anxiety is attitude. If you expect anxiety and failure, you are more likely to experience them. A positive attitude can go a long way. Test anxiety can be reduced if these negative thoughts can be replaced by constructive positive thoughts. Tell yourself that you are prepared and ready and that you have confidence in your abilities. Sometimes repeating positive statements can help during the test. Focus on reducing the negative and worrisome thoughts that provoke anxiety. Students who are anxious about tests tend to say things that are negative or exaggerated. Counter negative thoughts by thinking about more rational responses.

EZ-STEP-BY-STEP METHOD: Apply the following steps to transform negative thoughts into positive thoughts.

STEP 1: Awareness: First, look at your attitude – you must first become aware of your own thoughts.

STEP 2: Transformation: If there are any negative thoughts – rationalize and replace them with positive constructive self-talks.

STEP 3: Ignore: If there are still some traces of negative thoughts in your mind – do not dwell on them.

STEP 4: Affirmative: Approach your test – with a positive outlook.

Avoid negative thoughts and induce positive thoughts by doing the following:
- Avoid thinking of yourself in irrational or negative terms.
- Avoid negative and irrational thoughts about catastrophic results.
- Counter negative thoughts with other, more rational and positive thoughts.
- Completely eliminate any negative thoughts from your mind.

SELF-TALK: AFFIRMATIONS:

Research shows that everybody talks to themselves during a test. It will be often helpful to become aware of what you say to yourself. However, test anxious individuals say more negative things to themselves. The self-talk of test-anxious students almost always tends to be negative and self-defeating. Non-test anxious individuals say more positive things to themselves during the test and more helpful hints. Try to change what you say to yourself to more positive or helpful hints. Stop any negative thoughts and change them to more positive ones as soon as they kick in.

NEGATIVE THOUGHT STOPPING:

If you are experiencing test stress, it is likely that you are thinking negatively. Stop and interrupt the negative thoughts. It has been well documented that negative and frightening thoughts increase your anxiety and increase your physical symptoms of anxiety.

Negative thoughts are generally the starting point of stress and test related anxiety. So you have to deal firmly with those negative thoughts. Negative thought stopping can help reduce test anxiety before, during and after an exam. Thought stopping involves listening to your negative thoughts. Be aware of what you are saying to yourself, and stop saying it. You should immediately stop any negative thoughts as soon as you become aware of them and before they impair performance. It won't help you to do better; it will only interfere with your thinking.

You don't have to convince yourself that you are doing fine; just convince yourself to stop scaring yourself to death. On becoming aware of negative thoughts during a test situation, you can say, "stop" quietly to yourself and then say something positive. Sometimes it also helps to add a physical cue in preventing negative thoughts. You might want to pinch your finger lightly, slap your leg lightly, or shake your head lightly, when you say stop - to get your attention - anything to add a physical stimulus to your mental one. Also remind yourself that you can't afford any negative thoughts. This action as well as the definite decision not to harbor any negative thoughts will reinforce your decision.

NEGATIVE SELF-DEFEATING STATEMENTS TO POSITIVE SELF-FULFILLING STATEMENTS:

From Pessimism to Optimism: Continue to rephrase your worries in a positive manner. Every time you have a negative thought, write it down and then contradict it. As you practice this technique, you will begin to become a positive thinker. Negative thoughts have a way of turning into negative actions. So practice positive thinking.

Following are some of the negative thoughts that may pop up in your head while taking the test, replace them by reinforcing the positive thoughts, given below them to counter anxiety:

(A) WORRY ABOUT PERFORMANCE:

Negative: I don't think I have studied enough and I am not at all prepared for the test.
Positive: I have studied very hard and I am well prepared for the test.

Negative: I feel out of control, and I can't seem to remember any of the concepts I had learned.

Positive: I feel in control of myself, and if I take a deep breath, I will remember all that I have studied.

Negative: I have not studied enough and I do not know the test format, content, and strategies.
Positive: I do understand the test format, content, and strategies very well.

Negative: I can never finish this test on time and hence I will get a bad score.
Positive: If I follow my pacing strategy correctly, I should be able to finish the majority of my test on time and even if I miss a few questions, that's fine, I will work on improving my speed for the next time I take the test.

Negative: These questions are so hard that I don't even know from where to start.
Positive: These questions are a little tricky but I know how to crack them with the proven test-taking strategies that I have learned.

Negative: I feel overly nervous and I don't know how to get rid of my anxiousness.
Positive: If I try one of my relaxation techniques, I will feel calm, composed, and collected.

Negative: I will not get a good score and my family and friends will really be disappointed in me.
Positive: I will get a good score and my family and friends will be proud of me.

Negative: Question #7 is really hard and if I can't find the correct answer, this will really trip me up.
Positive: If I can't find the correct answer to question #7 – it's just one question, I can skip it, answer rest of the questions and maybe come back to it later.

(B) WORRY ABOUT PHYSICAL REACTIONS:

Negative: I feel sick; I'll never be able to get through the test.
Positive: I feel alright; I can pull through the test.

Negative: I'm sweating all over and my hands are shaking.
Positive: I'll be alright once I take a time out to close my eyes and relax for a bit.

(C) WORRY ABOUT HOW OTHERS ARE DOING:

Negative: I am going to do much worse on this test than anyone else here.
Positive: I am going to do much better on this test than anyone else here.

Negative: I'm going to be the last one done again, I must be really stupid.
Positive: I may be the last one done, but I will answer all questions to the best of my ability.

(D) WORRY ABOUT POSSIBLE NEGATIVE CONSEQUENCES:

Negative: This test is the most important test of my life and it will permanently affect my life.
Positive: This test is only one of the tests I will be taking and it will not permanently affect my life.

Negative: If I don't do well on this test, I'll never get a good score; if I don't get a good score, I'll never make it to a college of my choice; if I don't make it to college, I'll never be able to get a good job to make it a success.
Positive: I'm going to try my best to get a good score on this test; if I don't get a very good score on this test, I can still get into a decent college and get a reasonable good job, or I can always get experience, study more, and take the test again and get the score I deserve.

REMIND YOURSELF:
- Remind yourself that the test is only a small part of your academic life, and that your entire future does not depend on this test's outcome.
- Remind yourself that you've studied hard, you are well-prepared, and are going to do your best and be successful.
- Remind yourself that there will be other tests in life – this is not the last or the only one, there will be many others.

- Remind yourself of past successes – if you did well on your last test, you can do well on the upcoming test as well, and if you didn't do well on your last test, it need not necessarily predict your future prospects.
- Remind yourself that everything will be fine because you're doing your best.
- Remind yourself that you will probably experience some anxiety during the test, but the anxiety won't hamper your performance because you've practiced controlling the anxiety.
- Test can sometime be an intimidating word – use the word "quiz" rather than "exam" or "test" when you think about the upcoming test.

5.5: THE RIGHT CONFIDENCE:

BE CONFIDENT:

Your confidence level also plays a very important role while you are taking the test. A more confident mood will generate better concentration and performance.

(A) Don't be Under-confident: Being under-confident is not good for you since that can lead to extreme nervousness.

(B) Don't be Overconfident: Being overconfident is not good for you either, since that can lead to making careless and silly mistakes.

Therefore, don't be under-confident, or overconfident, just be confident.

SELF-CONFIDENCE:

Self-confidence feeds on itself, and unfortunately, so does the opposite of confidence - self-doubt. Sense of self-confidence in your ability leads to quick, more accurate answers, and it also results in a higher concentration level that yields more points. If you lack confidence, you won't be able to have a good concentration level, and you may end up reading question stems and answer choices several times, more times than you should, to the point where over-reading will confuse you and throw you off track. Remember, lower confidence level will lower your concentration level, which will in turn lead to shortage of time – and all this will increase your anxiety level.

Approach the exam with confidence: View the exam as an opportunity to show how much you've studied and to receive a reward for the studying you've done.

DON'T BE NERVOUS:

Being nervous is natural, and may be inevitable while taking any test. Nevertheless, don't let that nervousness get you down. In fact let that nervousness work to your advantage. It is indeed nice to be a little nervous. A little bit of nervousness will keep you alert and focused. However, too much of nervousness can result in losing concentration and making silly mistakes, and that can seriously affect your performance on the test. Therefore, don't be overly nervous, little bit of nervousness is natural and works to your advantage.

STAY ALERT & FOCUSED:

(A) Stay Alert: Make sure that you are alert while taking the test so that you perform at your best ability. Losing attention can very seriously affect your performance on the test.

(B) Stay Focused: Research shows that students who do well on tests think more about the test itself while test anxious students focus more on their feelings about the test. Try to stay positive and focus on the test itself and not on your feelings about the test. Concentrate on the task at hand and tell yourself that you will deal with your feelings. Get fully involved with answering the questions and block everything else out.

Don't be Distracted: Don't let your mind wander or get distracted; just give the test your complete undivided attention. Fight the urge to become preoccupied and distracted by thoughts and concerns unrelated to the test content.

Don't Think About Anything Other Than the Test: Try not to think about anything except the test, forget about everything else while taking the test. If you find yourself thinking about anything other than the test, just shake your head, discard that thought, and focus on your test.

STAY MOTIVATED:

Always remain motivated to study for your test and to take it. If you are motivated about learning the material, you are likely to remember the information. It is hard to remember material that doesn't interest you.

BE CAREFUL, NOT CARELESS:

You should be very careful while taking the test. You cannot afford to be careless and make silly mistakes. You may very well know how to answer a question correctly, but it would be very frustrating if you make small silly mistakes. Always remember, one small silly mistake can result in selecting an incorrect answer choice. In multiple choice questions, you don't get credit for your work; you only earn a point by selecting the correct answer choice. Double check your answer to avoid making silly mistakes. Often carelessness is our worst enemy while taking a test. Therefore, be very careful, and don't be careless.

TEST AVOIDANCE:

While there are some people who actually enjoy the opportunity and take pride in demonstrating their intelligence and expertise in the form of a good test score, majority of other people would do almost anything to prevent themselves from taking a test and going through the agony and that dreadful experience. Fortunately, there is good news for people who belong to the second group. There are things that any test-taker can do to make their test-taking experience at least little less nerve-wracking and a little more successful. If you work hard enough, you may even be able to transform into the first group of people who take pleasure in pitting themselves against the test writers, and not fall into their traps by cracking the test and coming out in the top percentile.

DON'T PANIC, REMAIN CALM:

It's vital that you remain cool, calm, composed, and collected during the test. Whether the questions are easy or hard, do not panic while answering the questions. If you panic, you may end up making silly and careless mistakes in answering even the easier questions incorrectly. The main secret to doing well on standardized tests is to remain calm and not panic, the sooner you realize this fact, the sooner you will become a pro at taking such tests.

5.6: HOW OTHER ELEMENTS AFFECT YOUR TEST ANXIETY:

DISCUSS YOUR ANXIETY WITH OTHERS:
- Share and express your test anxiety verbally or in writing openly and in a positive way with your friends, family, and instructors.
- Discuss thoroughly the purpose of your test and how it can help you progress academically.

HOW OTHERS CAN REDUCE YOUR ANXIETY:
- encourage you.
- remind you and praise you for your past achievements and performances.
- show confidence in you.
- remind you of your strengths.
- make you feel good about yourself.

UNWANTED ANXIETY: AVOID INTERACTING WITH ANXIOUS AND OBSESSIVE STUDENTS:
It is in your best interest to avoid interacting with or listening to anxious or obsessive students' right before you take the test. These kinds of people usually generate and instigate anxiety and tend to upset your stability and attitude. You should also avoid discussing any test content matter with your friends, just a few minutes before you enter the test center. Your friends may bring up some unimportant topic which you may have never heard about, or they may ask you a question to which you may or may not know the correct answer to, or they may sound overly well informed and prepared, or they may ask you something which you possibly overlooked. All this can completely throw you off of your confidence pedestal, and it can make you feel more nervous and less confident. So keep to yourself and focus on what you have learnt in a relaxed, composed manner. If you are sure that your friends will not talk about the test, then talking about other things may not negatively affect you. At this point, you have done whatever you could to prepare yourself, and any new information is not going to help you.
Consider the following points:
- Avoid talking with other students about the test content right before the test – their anxieties may rub off on you.
- Avoid talking with frightened test-anxious students' right before the test– anxiety is contagious.
- Avoid talking with panicky students who induce anxiety into others – they'll often be more confusing than helpful.
- Avoid talking with negative students – they will only increase your anxiety and may even make you doubt your knowledge.

DON'T LET ANY EXTERNAL FACTOR AFFECT YOUR PERFORMANCE:
You should not let any external factor, such as personal or work related problems affect your performance while taking the test. You should try to keep them at the back of your mind, and forget about everything else while taking the test; you will have all the time you need to think about them after the test. Moreover, thinking about your other problems while taking the test will neither solve them, nor will it help you answer the questions correctly. In fact thinking about them will make you lose your concentration, divert your mind, and of course you will also end up losing some very valuable time which you should have been spending on answering the test questions. Therefore, try not to let any external factor affect your performance, and just concentrate on your test.

CONCENTRATE ON YOUR OWN WORK, DON'T LOOK AT OTHERS:
You should concentrate on your own work and not look at how good or bad others are doing. Occasionally, you may find yourself stuck with a difficult question or a series of difficult questions, and at that point you may start looking around and see how everyone else is doing. You may then realize that everyone else is busy answering the questions. What you don't realize is the fact that those other students may be answering a different and an easier question, or they may just be trying to answer a question. You must also remember that everyone works at a different pace. Moreover, thinking about how well others are doing will not help you answer the question correctly. In fact, it can take away some valuable time, which you should be using on the test. Don't waste time worrying, doubting yourself, wondering how other people are doing, and blaming yourself. Don't get freaked out if other test-takers seem to be working more rapidly and frantically than you are. Don't make the mistake of assuming other people's alacrity as a sign of higher scores. Don't worry about what you should have done; pay attention to what you can do at the moment. Therefore, forget about everyone and everything else, and just concentrate on your work.

If given a choice, choose a seat in a corner: If you have an option of choosing your own seat in the test center – choose a seat in a corner with few distractions, probably near the front. However, that is not a choice for most standardized tests.

DON'T PANIC ON MENTAL BLOCKS:
If you experience any lapse of memory or mental block on a question, you should not let that throw you off into a panic mode. Such lapses of memory or mental blocks are perfectly normal and often temporary. Instead of wasting too much time on that question, you should simply leave that question for a while and return to it at a later time. You should try to get into a test alert and calm mode instead of a tense and anxious mode. You should not be stressed or tense about anything while taking the test.

MOMENTARY DISTRACTION CAN HELP:
Sometimes, momentary distractions can prove to be quite useful, but its effect may only be temporary and may not last for too long. If you are feeling extremely anxious, try distracting your tense mind by breaking or sharpening your pencil lead, or by switching to a new pen/pencil, or perhaps asking the proctor a superfluous question, if allowed.

TEST MOMENTUM:
For many students, the initial start of the test causes the greatest anxiety. The first 15-20 minutes of the test is valuable time that you should not waste.

THIS PAGE HAS BEEN INTENTIONALLY LEFT BLANK.

PART 6.0: THE TEST COUNTDOWN:

TABLE OF CONTENTS:

THIS PAGE HAS BEEN INTENTIONALLY LEFT BLANK.

6.1: MONTHS BEFORE TEST DAY:

TEST FORMAT – FIND OUT EACH & EVERY TEST DETAIL:
The very first thing you should do is to find out thoroughly each and every up-to-date test detail that you should know in order to better prepare yourself for the test.
- Test time for the entire test.
- Test time for each section.
- Number of sections.
- Number of questions in each section.
- Types of questions.
- Test structure – how many multiple choice and essay questions.
- How the test will be scored.
- If there is any penalty for incorrect answers.

FEEDBACK FROM OTHER STUDENTS:
The best way to get the feel of the actual test (other than reading our books) is to confer with other students to get their feedback on the test. Since they have already gone through what you are going through now, they may be able to give you some valuable feedback about how the actual test is going to be. Talk to them, interview them, and find out anything that may be helpful to you – such as types of questions, level of difficulty, test duration, test environment, etc. Also make sure to talk to several students, not just one, so that you're not influenced by only one person's experience. You should also try to talk to your teachers, mentors, and school counselors. Sometimes, they can provide useful advice based not only on their knowledge of the test but also on what they hear from thousands of students who have already taken such tests.

TEST DIRECTIONS & SAMPLE QUESTIONS:
(A) Don't Waste Time Reading Directions or Sample Questions: Do not waste any time in reading the directions or looking at the sample questions at the beginning of each section. You are expected to know them ahead of taking the test.

(B) Learn Test Directions in Advance: One of the easiest things you can do to save yourself some precious time on the actual test is to understand the test directions that appear at the beginning of each section completely and thoroughly ahead of taking the test so that you can skip them during the test and save some very valuable time. While taking the actual test, just skim the directions or skip them all together. By doing this, you'll also be able to better prepare yourself for the test and will know what to expect on the test.

(C) Test Directions Almost Never Change: The directions given in our books and test booklets are identical to the directions you will see on the actual test. Learn these directions and format of each section ahead of taking the test. Since the directions normally never change and they are always exactly the same, there's absolutely no good reason to waste your time on the day of the test by reading them. Moreover, you'll feel more confident if you are already fully conversant with the directions.

(D) Different Test Sections May Have Different Test Directions: Since the test directions are not constant for all sections of the test and since different test sections may have different test directions, make sure you learn the directions for each section so that you don't end up mixing them up.

(E) Skim Through the Test Directions: Nevertheless, it is always a good idea to briefly skim through the directions for a few seconds (less than 10 seconds), without spending too much time reading them.

(F) How Much Time will you Save? While this advice may seem petty, if you do the math, you can end up saving quite a bit of time. For instance, let's say you have six different sections/formats, and if it takes about two minutes to read the directions and sample questions for each format, that's a total of twelve minutes. Now, you can either spend those twelve minutes in reading the directions and sample problems (something that you can easily avoid) and earn zero points, or spend those precious twelve minutes in answering at least six to ten questions and potentially earn some good points that count towards your score. We think the decision is simple – save these 12 precious minutes, skim the directions for 12 seconds, and spend this time in answering 12 actual test questions.

PLAN YOUR TEST DATE:

One of the first important decisions you'll need to make is when to take the test. Although, this may seem simpler than it actually is, there are several factors to consider, such as the ones given below:

(A) Test Locations: Find when the test is being offered close to where you live.

(B) Application Deadlines: Find the deadline of each college or scholarship agency you're interested in applying, so that they can have your score before the cut-off dates. You'll have enough time to decide which college to select among the ones which accepted you.

(C) Research: You'll need some extra time finding more information about the colleges that have accepted you and to ultimately make the decision about your final choice. You'll also need time to do some research and visit a few college campuses.

(D) Coursework: Consider where you stand in your coursework. If you're taking some Math/English courses, it may be a good idea for you to take the test once you complete these courses so that those subjects are still fresh in your memory.

(E) Re-testing: If you're planning to take the test more than once in order to improve your scores, you should plan your test-date in such a manner that you have enough time to retake the test, just in case you are not satisfied with your test scores. So plan on taking your test far ahead of your application deadline so that you have an opportunity to take the test more than once, should the need arise and if you feel your scores don't accurately reflect your true ability level. Most schools/colleges take your best score and not the most recent or average score. Also, some schools/colleges take the best of your math, verbal, quantitative, and analytical scores, even if they were not on the same test.

You should definitely consider re-testing under the following circumstances:

- You aren't satisfied with your scores and you don't think they accurately represent your true abilities.
- You see a huge discrepancy between your practice test scores and your actual test scores.
- You had some technical problems during the test, such as misunderstanding the directions, running out of time, etc.
- You had some personal problems during the test, such as you were ill or you were seriously worried about personal matters that came in your way of performing well.
- You have taken and completed some coursework or test-prep course, or gone through an intensive review since you last tested.

If you don't have one of the reasons listed above, and if you take the test again, most likely you'll end up getting almost the same scores or you may even see a slight decline in your test scores. However, if you do have one of the points listed above, you may see an improvement in your test scores.

TEST SCHEDULE:

For Computer Tests:

- Schedule the test according to your best time of the day. When you sign up to take the test on a specific date, you will be given a choice of time slots. Some people are morning people while others work well in the mid-afternoon. Consider how your energy and alertness levels vary during the course of a day. Also, consider possible transportation problems, such as rush hours. With these and other relevant factors in mind, select the time slot that works best for you.
- Allow yourself enough time for the test. For instance, if you sign up to take the test at 10:00 A.M., do not make a doctor's appointment for 8:00 A.M. or 12:00 noon. If you go to the doctor's at 8:00 A.M., you may run late to take your test; and if you make a 12:00 appointment, you can't possibly get there on time, and you'll just spend the latter half of the test worrying about it.

6.2: THE WEEK BEFORE TEST DAY:

THE FINAL COUNTDOWN:

The final countdown has begun. This is the week before the test day, which means your test is right around the corner. It may appear as if your whole life depends on this test. You've planned it for years, agonized for months, and by now you have spent at least a few weeks or months in intensive preparation.

AVOID PRE-TEST JITTERS:

As the test approaches closer and closer, your anxiety level may also rise higher and higher. Don't worry and calm any pre-test jitters, this is normal. You test preparation is at its peak. The butterflies in your stomach have gone ballistic. Your thinking is getting cloudy. Your nervousness is at an all time high. Your anxiety is rising by the hour. Maybe you think you are not ready. Maybe you think you don't know your stuff. You start doubting yourself. Almost every test-taker goes through the same thing. All this can very easily set you off to a panic mode. But, calm down, don't freak out. We have the remedy. Equipped with the study material that you've learned from our books, you have the best tools available to take your test head-on. Follow our advice on how to control your anxiety and stress – before and during the test.

TAPER OFF YOUR TEST-PREP:

Get ready for the final countdown. Some of the best test-takers study less and less as the test approaches. A week before your test date, start tapering off your study time and try to take it easy. It is paramount that you must complete your review/learning process a week before the actual test date. During the final week, just review what you've learned in your entire preparation process. Look back over your preparation and give yourself credit for how far you've come. You have worked very hard on your test preparation and it's almost over. All your hard work is finally going to pay off soon! Just don't lose your stamina now – do whatever it takes to keep going until you come out of that test room with a sense of pride and look of accomplishment on your face.

Positive self-talk can be extremely therapeutic and stimulating, especially as the test date approaches. Tell yourself all sorts of positive things such as, how hard you have worked, and how well you are going to do. Substitute any negative thoughts with affirming and assuring statements that boost your energy and confidence. Accentuate the positives and suppress the negatives! Your confidence level, attitude, and outlook are the key to your success on the test.

Remember, your test is like a marathon, and you are like a runner. Even runners don't run a marathon the day before the real thing, so even you shouldn't do that!

6.3: THE DAY BEFORE THE TEST:

FINAL REVIEW:

On the day before the test, just do a final review of key notes on your review sheets. Do not get into any details or learn anything completely new that you have never studied before. Try to avoid doing intensive studying the day before the test. At this point, there's very little that you can do to help yourself. The best you can do is to review what you've learned during your entire test-prep period. By this time, your brain will be running on overdrive, and it will need some space to sink in all the content that you have learned so far. We recommend that you don't indulge in any massive review or take a full-length practice test if you have fewer than 48 hours left before the actual test date. Doing so will probably do more harm than good. It will likely hurt your score on the actual test for more than one reason. Cramming at this time would lead to cluttering your brain. It will induce stress, and you may just wind up exhausting yourself and burning out.

TIME OFF:

By this time, if you've studied hard, you've done everything you possibly could. Whatever you've learned is already firmly stored in the hard drive of your memory. Try not to think too much about the test and keep the test out of the realm of your consciousness; watch TV, do some light work-out, or simply relax. It will be advantageous for you to store your physical and mental resources for up to 24 hours. On the test day, you will be able to perform better if you allow your brain some well deserved downtime. This is the time to relax and give yourself some time off so that you store all your energy for the BIG day! Even racehorses are rested like royalty the night before the final race.

6.4: THE NIGHT BEFORE THE TEST:

HAVE A HEALTHY DINNER:

You should try to eat a healthy and nutritious dinner, which is rich in proteins and other essential vitamins. A high carbohydrate dinner will also give you extra energy that you may need to sit for long hours in the test room and deal with test anxiety and nervousness while taking the test. Good nutritious food will help you focus and think with clarity. Eat plenty of fruits and vegetables, low-fat protein such as fish, skinless poultry, beans, and legumes, and whole grains such as brown rice, or multi-grain breads, and pastas. Stay away from junk food or lots of sugary, salty, heavy, or high-fat greasy food.

DO NOT STAY UP AND STUDY ALL NIGHT BEFORE THE TEST DATE:

Our advice is not to do any studying at or after this point. By this time, you have done your best to prepare yourself for the test; any extra studying all night will not translate into a higher score. If you don't know the material by now, it's probably too late. In fact, sleep deprivation can lead to panic, sleepiness, and fatigue during the test. So don't clutter your mind by studying until the last minute. To be able to perform to the best of your best ability, it is very important to be awake and relaxed. You are more likely to recall more of what you have learned if you are awake and alert than if you are tired and sleepy.

RELAX BEFORE GOING TO SLEEP:

As the night progresses, relax and get plenty of rest the evening/night before your test. You may do some relaxation exercises such as reading a good book, watching some TV, but nothing too tiring or stressful.

SLEEP EARLY AND HAVE A GOOD NIGHT'S SLEEP:

Make sure you sleep early and get a reasonably adequate amount of good night's sleep before the test so that you are well rested, relaxed, energized, and alert in the morning while taking the test. Sleepiness, fatigue, tiredness, restlessness, or lack of attention can seriously affect your performance on the test, and you will not be able to function at your absolute best. You should leave yourself some extra time in the morning. Therefore, stay relaxed, rested, and awake, and when you arrive at the test center, you will feel at ease and rested so that you can perform at your optimum potential!

CHANGE YOUR SLEEP CYCLE LONG BEFORE YOUR TEST DATE:

Consider your usual sleep pattern and follow the same schedule on the night before the test. If you all of a sudden go to bed much earlier than your body is used to, you may find yourself tossing and turning for hours, or if you go to bed much later than your body is used to, you may find yourself short of sleep. Either way, you'll be more tired than you would have been if you had followed your usual sleep pattern.

For instance, if you are used to going to bed at 11:00 p.m. and getting 7 hours of sleep, go ahead and follow the same routine the night before the test. Do not think that if you go to bed at 9:00 p.m. the day before the test, those extra two hours will help you. More than likely, you will wake up two hours earlier and this will cause you more anxiety and a tendency to be more tired during the test. Moreover, oversleeping may sometimes lead to headaches. On the other hand, don't be awake until 2:00 a.m., which may result in sleep deprivation.

However, all this may vary from person to person, so it may be a good idea to try sleeping earlier and longer, or later and shorter, not just the night before the test but a few days prior to the test. It's hard for most people to fall asleep earlier or later than they're used to. Depending on what your test time is, you should make an effort to change your sleep cycle that matches your test time long before your test date so that you get accustomed to it.

SET UP AN ALARM:

Set up an alarm, leaving enough time for you to get up and get ready. Set a back-up system for your alarm clock, such as a second alarm and/or arrange for a wake up call from a friend. It may be a good idea to ask someone to call you to wake you up, just to make sure that you are up on time and you don't oversleep the morning of the test.

6.5: THE MORNING OF THE TEST:

CLOTHES TO WEAR FOR THE TEST:

(A) Dress in Comfortable Clothes: Choose comfortable, informal clothing. This is not the time to make a fashion statement; comfort, not style, should be the order of the day. Since you're going to be sitting in the same place for several hours, make sure to dress in comfortable clothes which allow for movement. It only makes sense to wear something you're especially comfortable in so that it helps you relax better and concentrate more on the test. For many people, what they're wearing can have a big impact on how they feel about themselves. If you happen to be one of those, pick something you like and feel good wearing it so that you can get that extra boost of confidence. And make sure to set your clothes out ahead of time so you don't stress about it on the morning of the test.

(B) Dress in Layered Clothes: For maximum comfort, you should dress in layered clothing. By doing so, you'll easily be able to adjust to the test room's temperature by taking off a layer or adding another layer depending on the temperature of the room. Definitely bring a sweater or a jacket with you. It is important that you don't feel too cold or too warm while taking the test, because that may cause physical discomfort to you, and that can seriously affect your performance on the test.

LIGHT BREAKFAST IN THE MORNING:

(A) Eat Healthy: Make sure you eat a light to moderate, healthy, and high nutrition breakfast in the morning before the test. Try to make it something filling but not anything too heavy or greasy. A good choice would be cereal, fruit, bagels, toast, or eggs.

(B) Eat What You are Used To: You should select the healthiest breakfast that you are used to having. If you usually have a very light breakfast, choose your best light breakfast. For instance, if you usually have a piece of toast and a glass of juice, you probably shouldn't have a loaded omelet and a heavy milkshake. Similarly, if you usually have a very heavy breakfast, make sure to choose something significant but not too heavy or greasy. Either way, you should not skip breakfast altogether or eat significantly less or more than you're used to. And don't try anything entirely new, this is not the time to experiment with new cuisines or recipes.

(C) Don't Overeat, Don't be Hungry: Don't under-eat or eat so little that you have an empty stomach and stay hungry throughout your test. Overeating or hunger can seriously affect your performance on the test. A healthy body leads to a healthy and active mind.

(D) Avoid Sugar: A sweet sugary breakfast will most likely do more harm than good. While it may give you an initial boost of energy to start your day, that energy will most likely burn off before you even realize it. Hence, avoid donuts, pastries, or anything else with a lot of sugar/fat in it.

(E) Caffeine Note: Unless you are absolutely addicted to caffeine, it's a good idea to stay away from having coffee or sodas. So, don't drink a lot of coffee if you're not used to it; too much caffeine may make you jittery, agitated, restless, and overly nervous. Also, keep in mind that even though you have coffee every day, having coffee on a normal day is different from having it on the test day. Contrary to popular belief, coffee won't make you more alert; instead, it's more likely to further increase your anxiety level. According to research, test-takers with coffee consumption (even if they are caffeine-addicted) are more likely to lose their focus somewhere during the test, but there is no data that indicates any sort of alertness problems without coffee consumption. A good substitute for coffee or soda may be fresh juice or fat-free flavored milk.
Note: Sugar and caffeine do not enhance your test-taking performance. Your consumption should depend upon your habits and tolerance level, which may differ from person to person.

SAY NO TO DRUGS:

Using drugs (prescription or recreational), particularly to prepare for and take a big test is absolutely self-defeating. Don't be fooled by any advice which suggests test performance improvement. This is all a gimmick. Moreover, if they're illegal drugs, you may wind up with a bigger problem than the test on your hands. There is no good reason to try such drugs. Most of these drugs have many side-effects and disadvantages; the only advantage is the placebo effect, which too is not far reaching.

TEST DAY WARM-UP:

It's important to warm-up your brain before you take the test. Read something like a newspaper or a magazine. You really don't want, "Your time starts now!" to be the first written text your brain tries to assimilate that day. As you travel to the test center, review your key notes. Not only will it give you a quick refresher, but will also put you in the right mindset for the test – both of which are very important.

6.6: DURING THE TEST:

BE READY FOR A MARATHON:

Think of preparing for your test as a marathon or training for an athletic event and the test day as the last lap. Once you've done your best to train and prepare yourself, give it everything you learned and give it nothing less than your absolute best. The test day is going to be a long day. If you add up the total test time, including travel time, break time, and the administrative tidbit, you're looking at an experience of three to four hours or possibly more. But when you come out of that test room with a sense of pride and the unstoppable smile of joy on your face, you'll know that every second of that long marathon was worth it!

PANIC STRATEGY FOR HANDLING STRESS WHILE WAITING FOR THE TEST:

On the day of the test, while you're waiting for the test to begin, it's normal to find yourself a little anxious or nervous. There is nothing wrong with that, in fact, most test-takers feel that way. Now, how you handle these pre-test jitters may affect your performance on the test.

TEST CENTER RULES & REGULATIONS:

Listen carefully and follow the rules and instructions given by the test supervisor/proctor at the beginning of the test. The proctor may give you some valuable information just before handing out the test, so don't miss them. These may sound like those boring airline instructions that you hear upon every landing and take-off. Most likely, you may already be aware of those instructions, but it never hurts to be reminded of them again. Moreover, this is the time when you should drop any external thoughts and concentrate completely on the test.

Note: If you do not follow these rules and instructions, you may be dismissed from the test center and your scores may be cancelled.

FILL OUT ACCURATE INFORMATION ON THE ANSWER SHEET:

Make sure to carefully fill out accurate information on your answer sheet such as your name, address, social security number, date of birth, etc. The same information that you enter on your answer sheet will be printed on your score reports. Any wrong information entered on the answer sheet may cause a delay and/or cancellation of your scores. Pay attention to the directions given by the test supervisor/proctor for filling out the answer sheet. After you are done with the administrative stuff, it's time for the real stuff – it's show-time!

DEFECTIVE MATERIAL:

If something is technically wrong, such as a defective test booklet where few pages are stuck together or the ink has faded out or if you are taking the test on the computer and there is something wrong with the software or hardware of the computer – don't panic, just raise your hand and tell the proctor about the problem. The test supervisor will take care of your problem promptly.

ASK FOR CLARIFICATIONS:

If you have any questions about the test directions, procedures, etc., do not hesitate to ask about any aspect of the test-taking procedures that are not clear to you from the test supervisor or proctor. It is always better to be clear than to take the test with some doubts in your mind. Test center staff will be available throughout the test. If you have any questions about the administrative part of the test (not about the contents of the test or questions), simply raise your hand and one of the test proctors will attend to your query.

MEMORY RETRIEVAL:

If there are any important formulas or rules that you really need to know and you think they are most likely going to be on the test, and you are scared that you may forget them, or you are not confident enough that you'll be able to retrieve them from your memory when they may be needed in a question, it may be a good idea for you to write down those items on the back of your test booklet or the scratch paper. If you ever need that information in any of the questions, you will have it available right in front of you and you won't have to stretch or rely on your memory. Make sure that you don't spend more than a few seconds doing this exercise and that you only note down very hard to remember critical information.

PANIC STRATEGY FOR HANDLING STRESS DURING THE TEST:

On the day of the test, before you begin your test, promise yourself that you will do your absolute best, and try to remember that pledge throughout the test. If you are in the middle of the test and you're under pressure, and something happens unexpectedly, like an unusually tricky question, it can easily upset you and put you in a panic mode. You'll see your confidence slipping away. Panic ignites nervousness and confusion, which may further leave you feeling helpless and discouraged.

Don't let one bad question ruin an entire section. Likewise, don't let your performance on one section ruin your performance on the other. Remember, one bad question or a bad performance on one section will not completely ruin your score unless you did really poorly on almost every question. Although, being disturbed due of one crazy question can have a cumulative negative effect which may significantly ruin your performance on the other sections. Missing a few points here and there won't do as much damage as losing your balance will.

You must have an emergency strategy to deal with such panic that might arise in the middle of the test and get it under control so that you again get back to the test.
- Remind yourself how hard you've studied and how well you've prepared for the test. You know the structure of the test, you know the format, you know the content, you know the strategies, and you've also practiced extensively using the EZ Solutions' books. You've no reason to lose it in the middle of the game; you must make every effort to keep your spirits up until the last question of the last section of the test.
- Take a short "time out" for 20 to 60 seconds. Close your eyes and put the test temporarily out of mind and sight.
- Try one of our techniques to relax yourself.
- Check your posture to make sure you're sitting straight up. If you find yourself stooping, it'll be hard to get enough oxygen in your lungs. You'll feel fresher when you have a balanced supply of oxygen going through your lungs to your brain.

TAKE SHORT BREAKS:
While taking the test, if you ever feel exhausted, utterly confused, blank, or overly nervous, you should take a break for a few seconds by sitting on your seat, closing your eyes, and taking deep breaths. This will clear up your cluttered head, take your mind away from the confusion, and give you the rest you need. You may be concerned that taking breaks may leave you with less time to finish your test. But what you don't realize is the fact that it is better to take a few short breaks for a few seconds whenever needed instead of taking the rest of the test with a cluttered mind. Therefore, short breaks can sometime prove to be very beneficial, feel free to make use of them if you feel comfortable doing so.

BREAK TIME:
Take advantage of breaks to go to the hallway for a small walk, grab a snack, and stretch your legs. At this time, don't listen to or discuss with other test-takers about the test, especially if they are talking about how easy or hard they find the test to be. Take some type of high energy nutritious snack/cold drink of water or beverage with you to eat/drink after each hour of test to keep your energy level up. This will also increase your concentration level and keep you from becoming drowsy.

6.7: AFTER THE TEST:

First and foremost, as soon as you get out of the test room, congratulate yourself!

Don't be surprised if you walk out of the test room thinking that you completely blew it. We can assure you that you are not the only one; in fact, many people, even some of the high scorers, feel that way. This is a pretty normal reaction. People tend to remember the questions that knocked them off, not the ones that they knocked off.

So, if you are having any negative thoughts, just ignore them. We're confident that you performed your best on the test and you were well prepared because you followed the EZ Solutions Program. So, be proud that you were well prepared and did your best.

Now, put the test in your distant memory. After all the hard-work that you've put in preparing for and taking the test, it's time to celebrate your success. Go watch a movie. Get together with friends. Relax. Have fun. Enjoy.

After all, you have every reason to celebrate. You worked very hard to prepare for the test. You performed your best. You're going to get a good score. You're going to get admitted into a great school of your choice. So, start thinking about all the great times and planning for your future academic career.

THIS PAGE HAS BEEN INTENTIONALLY LEFT BLANK.

PART 7.0: PLAN OF ATTACK ON TEST DAY:

TABLE OF CONTENTS:

THIS PAGE HAS BEEN INTENTIONALLY LEFT BLANK.

7.1: PLAN OF ATTACK – WHILE READING QUESTIONS:

READ THE QUESTIONS CAREFULLY: DON'T MISUNDERSTAND OR MISINTERPRET:
Don't misunderstand the question or misinterpret the information given and asked in the question. Make sure to read the questions carefully before you begin to answer them. Remember, some of the questions are worded in an indirect manner to trick you; be very careful of such questions. You should re-read the question if you are confused or having a problem understanding it. It's fairly easy to miss even the simplest question by reading carelessly and overlooking an important word or detail.

READ THE QUESTIONS COMPLETELY: DON'T READ A PART OF IT:
Make sure to read the questions completely before you begin to answer them. In order to make sure that you understand a question, you must read the question in its entirety and not just a part of it, even if you think you understand the question without reading it completely. The other part of the question which you did not read may have some pertinent information or something completely different than what you may have anticipated. You have the entire question at your disposal, so make use of it by reading it completely.

READ THE QUESTION AS IS: DON'T ADD, DELETE, OR CHANGE WORDS:
Never add, delete, or change words in a question. You must read the questions the way they are written, not the way you would like them to be in order to fit your answer. Even a subtle addition, deletion, or alteration of words in a question can change the complete meaning of a question, and by doing that, you would be answering something completely different than what is being asked in the question.

READ THE QUESTION AS NEEDED: DON'T UNDER-READ OR OVER-READ A QUESTION:
It is very important that you don't under-read or over-read a question. Often, simple looking questions are just what they appear to be, so don't read too much into them and make them look more complicated than what they actually are. Likewise, often, difficult looking questions are also just what they appear to be, so don't read too little into them and make them look easier than what they actually are. In both the cases, you will be misunderstanding the question and getting it wrong. Therefore, understand the question properly before you try to solve it, and don't read too much or too little into any question; just read into the question what's right for that particular question.

REPHRASE THE QUESTION IF NEEDED:
Some questions are straightforward and don't really require too much time or effort in interpreting them. However, some questions are not straightforward and are often indirect, complex, wordy, or convoluted, and which contain difficult words and/or double negatives. They are often worded in a tricky and confusing manner. Expressing those difficult or confusing questions in your own words can prove to be quite helpful. Therefore, before beginning to answer the question, rephrase or restate the question in your own words in a way that makes sense to you. Rephrasing the question can make it clearer to you, but be careful not to change the meaning of the question.

DON'T SKIP OR RANDOM GUESS QUESTIONS WITHOUT READING THEM:
Always read the questions before you choose to skip or random guess them. Every question at least deserves to be read before you decide to attempt, skip, or random guess it. It would be very frustrating if you skip a question without reading it and later realizing that it was an easy question and you could have answered it correctly. Therefore, give each and every question a fair chance before you decide to skip or random guess them.

Finally, make sure you understand exactly what the question asks for and what you need to do in order to answer it correctly in the minimum possible time. If the question is not clear or if you are confused, reread the question.

7.2: PLAN OF ATTACK – WHILE ANSWERING QUESTIONS:

WARM-UP & SET THE MOMENTUM: FIRST ANSWER A FEW VERY EASY QUESTIONS:

You should start your test with first answering a few very easy questions that you know best. Doing so will give you an opportunity, ability, and the endurance to "warm-up" for answering the more difficult questions. This will put you in a confident state of mind, reduce your anxiety, and set up the momentum of the test. It will also help you build confidence, score points, and mentally orient yourself to vocabulary, concepts, and may also help you make associations with more difficult questions. Nothing can be worse than getting your very first couple of questions wrong; this can very seriously hamper your confidence level. This suggestion is true for both, paper-based tests and computer-based tests. Most paper-based tests are organized in order of difficulty, and most computer-based tests start with a medium-difficulty question and progress based on your response. So you don't have to make any effort to follow this suggestion, just answer the questions as they come to you. Therefore, first answer a couple of extremely easy questions before moving on to other questions.

DON'T PICK AN ANSWER ONLY BECAUSE IT IS FACTUALLY TRUE:

Just because an answer choice is factually true does not necessarily mean that it is the correct answer. You should not pick an answer choice just because it is factually true; also make sure that it answers the question that has been asked. Problems may also arise when you encounter something in a test question that contradicts facts or actual practice. In such a situation, you must ignore the facts or actual practice and answer the question on the basis of what is given in the test question. For instance, you may think that George Washington was the greatest president of the United States. Now, this is probably your personal opinion, according to the test question, maybe Abraham Lincoln was the greatest president of the United States. So don't let your opinion affect your decision in choosing your correct answer.

BEWARE OF PARTIALLY CORRECT ANSWER CHOICES:

Beware of answer choices that are half correct or partly correct. Sometimes an answer choice may have an element which seems to be correct, but it may have another element that makes the whole statement incorrect. So be very careful not to fall in the traps of partially correct answer choices. Read each answer choice completely before making your final choice. For instance, an answer choice may state that George Washington was the first president of the United States who introduced the civil rights. Now, the first portion of the answer is correct, but the other portion makes the whole statement false.

BEWARE OF PREMATURELY CORRECT ANSWER CHOICES:

Beware of answer choices that are prematurely or preliminarily correct. Sometimes, questions require multiple steps, and the answer to each intermediate step may often be included as answer choices. If you make the mistake of reading these questions too fast without realizing what exactly is being asked, you can easily make the mistake of choosing an answer choice that corresponds to an intermediate step, which is not the correct answer to the question. For instance, you may be given a complex algebraic equation with an unknown variable x. Now, you may be smart enough to crack the question and find the correct value of x; however, the question may have asked you to find the value of x^2.

READ ALL ANSWER CHOICES BEFORE MAKING YOUR SELECTION:

Make sure to read all answer choices before making your final selection. Often times, some questions include answer choices that seem credible but aren't quite the correct ones. It is very common to experience a situation where the very first answer choice may look tempting to you; however, the correct or best answer may be farther down the list. So always read all the answer choices just to be sure, especially on the verbal section where two or more choices may look correct but only one of them is the best one.

NEVER RELY ON OUTSIDE INFORMATION:

Answer questions based only on the information provided, and not on what you think you already know. Using any outside knowledge or using what you already know about the topic may facilitate your understanding and speed up your comprehension process, but it should not be used or presumed as additional given information. Interpret the questions literally and at their face value. When answering test questions, you must base your answer solely on the information contained in the test question. Remember, using outside knowledge may even work against your interests.

DON'T PICK AN ANSWER JUST BECAUSE IT'S TEMPTING:

You should not pick an answer just because it is complex or looks good. These distracters are answer choices that may look right but aren't quite right. They are purposely thrown in by the test makers to tempt you to pick them, and it's fairly easy to pick them if you haven't read the question carefully or understood it clearly. So be very careful of distracters and don't pick an answer based on how they look.

ANSWER THE QUESTION ASKED:

Always make sure that you are answering the question asked and not the one you thought was going to be asked. In other words, don't answer the wrong question with the incorrect answer! The best way to make sure that you are answering the question being asked and avoid answering the question that you thought was being asked is to underline or circle what you have been asked for, or what you have been asked to solve for. When you find the answer, make sure that is what was being asked for. Sometimes you may think you have found the answer, but you may have to do another step to get what was actually being asked for in the question. For instance, a math question may require you to solve an equation in order to get the correct answer, but instead of asking for the value of x or the unknown, the question may instead ask for the value of $2x$ or $(x - 7)$.

RESEMBLANCE OF AN ACTUAL TEST QUESTION WITH A PREVIOUSLY SEEN QUESTION:

Same but Different Questions: Be particularly careful answering questions that closely resemble questions you've seen before in your practice exercises, samples tests, or even on one of the previous tests. You must realize there are only limited numbers of concepts that test makers test and retest but in a somewhat different way, over and over again. These are modified versions of the same questions and they basically follow the same basic patterns, modifying questions sometimes slightly and other times significantly. Only the words and numbers change, which makes every question unique in Itself; and they all pretty much use the same concepts, which makes all questions quite similar. There are some basic underlying concepts which appear on every test, such as the Pythagorean Theorem in the math section and subject-verb agreement in the verbal section. Hence, you may often come across questions that are very similar to or resemble very closely the ones you have previously seen, but they may in fact be different questions and may also have different correct answers. Don't make the mistake of assuming that you already know the answer just because the question looks familiar to you. Always read every question carefully and don't let slight changes in wording catch you off guard.

NEVER MAKE UNWANTED ASSUMPTIONS:

Never make unwanted assumptions on any of the test questions in any section of the test. You should not assume anything other than what is given in the question and/or what can be concluded from the information provided in the question. It would be improper to make any unwanted assumption that is not given or can't be inferred from the information given in the question.

RELY ON YOUR KNOWLEDGE AND DON'T WATCH FOR PATTERNS:

There are many myths associated with multiple choice tests that their correct answers follow patterns. The most popular myth is that there will never be more than two questions with the same lettered answer following each other. Another one is that if you haven't chosen a certain letter answer for the last few questions then the answer to the next one would be that letter. Noticing that all of the last four consecutive questions had an answer "C" or they were "A, B, C, and D", is not at all a good reason to be doubtful of your knowledge and change your answers. Dismiss all such myths as there is no scientific truth to any of these myths. You should always rely on your knowledge and not watch for answer patterns. Select the answer that you think is correct based on your knowledge about the subject. The questions and their answers are randomly generated and therefore, it is almost impossible to predict any pre-set patterns or positions of the correct answer choices. Hence, it is always better to trust your knowledge to help you answer the questions.

ONE QUESTION MAY HELP IN ANSWERING ANOTHER:

Information given in one question may help you in another question. Use hints from questions you know to answer questions you do not know. Occasionally, you may find information relevant to one question, sometimes given away in another test question. So be alert and you may be able to use or apply the information given in one question, on another test question.

PAY ATTENTION TO INSTRUCTIONS GIVEN FOR A GROUP OF QUESTIONS:

There may be a diagram, chart, graph, or some type of special instructions given in the middle of the test that pertains to a specific group of questions. Be careful to note that you don't miss out on them and make sure that you apply those instructions to all the questions in that group. For instance, you may see something like: "For question 6-9, use the following diagram."

KNOW WHERE YOU ARE IN THE ORDER OF DIFFICULTY:

As you work your way through a section, realizing where you are in the order of difficulty and being aware of the level of each question can help you in many different ways. You'll be able to determine whether or not the answer to a question should be an obvious choice or not.

(A) Easy Questions: Easy questions are the questions that you are totally sure about, and confident that you can answer them easily. These questions can usually be answered very quickly and normally, they do not require too much of work and thinking. On these questions, it is fair to trust your first impulse. You don't have to be very suspicious; the answer probably should come quite easily. If an easy question is taking too much of your time or is taking too much of work and thinking, then you are thinking more than you need to or reading too much into it, and you probably are on a wrong track. Go back, re-read the question and the answer choices, and check if you made any incorrect assumptions or have fallen into a trap before answering too quickly. In most of the easy questions, the most obvious answer choice or the answer choice that strikes you immediately is normally the correct answer.

(B) Moderate/Medium Questions: Moderate/medium difficulty level questions are the questions that you think you can answer but would require some time and thinking. These questions usually take a little longer than the easy questions, and normally require some work and thinking. On these questions, your first hunch may or may not be right; the obvious answer may or may not be right. If a medium question is taking too little or too much of your time or is requiring too little or too much of work and thinking, then you are thinking less than or more than you need to or reading too little or too much into it, and you probably are on a wrong track. Go back, re-read the question and the answer choices, and check if you made any incorrect assumptions or have fallen into a trap by answering too quickly. In most of the medium questions, the most obvious answer choice or the answer choice that strikes you immediately may or may not be the correct answer.

(C) Difficult Questions: Difficult questions are the questions that you think you can answer but would require a lot of time and thinking, or you have no clue about them. Difficult questions are the questions that you are not at all sure about, and are not confident that you can do them. These questions usually take a lot longer than other questions, and normally require a lot of work and thinking. On these questions, it is fair not to trust your first impulse; the obvious answer is more likely to be wrong. You need to be more suspicious; the answer probably shouldn't come very easily. If a difficult question is taking too little of your time or is requiring too little work, then you are thinking less than you need to or reading too little into it, and you probably are on the wrong track. Go back, re-read the question and the answer choices, and check if you made any incorrect assumptions or have fallen into a trap by answering too quickly. In most of the difficult questions, the most obvious answer choice or the answer choice that strike you immediately is normally not the correct answer.

EXPERIMENTAL SECTION:

Experimental questions/sections do not count toward your scores. If you feel you've done extremely poorly on a section, it could very well be an experimental section. The experimental questions/sections often contain questions that are harder and weirder than the usual questions on the real sections. So, don't let an especially hard section throw you off. Don't think or try to figure out which questions/sections are un-scored or experimental. Obviously, some people try to figure out which section is experimental. As a matter of fact, some study guides advices that the questions in the experimental section are a little weird or unusual from the ordinary questions and you should try to identify it. Some even advice that most often the last section is the experimental section. Ignore all these advices; you really have no sure way to figure it out.

If you encounter a series of questions that seem strange to you, do your best. The test administrators want you to attempt the experimental section like any other scored section, and they do their best to keep you guessing. Now this is a chance that you have to decide if you would like to take. If you guess right, these experimental questions will not count and you have no reason to worry about them. However, if you guess wrong, these experimental questions will count and you could blow the whole test. It's a risky decision where the odds of losing are high, and therefore, we recommend you to treat all sections as scored sections unless you are told otherwise. The experimental section is designed to look like a real section, and there is no sure shot way to identify it. You really can't determine the Unidentified Experimental sections/questions. So don't waste any time trying to identify the experimental section. There is no way to know for sure which questions/sections won't count and your guess may very well be wrong. Wrongfully thinking that certain questions are experimental and not taking those questions seriously can completely throw off your score. You'll only end up wasting time. Instead, do your absolute best on every question of every section without worrying about whether it's experimental or not. Treat each question as if it counts and you'll be covered in either situation.

7.3: EZ METHOD TO ANSWERING QUESTIONS:

THINK, LOOK, ANSWER:

(A) Think: First, think and focus on formulating an answer that makes sense based on the facts given in the question, without the benefit of looking at the answer choices.

(B) Look: Then, once you have an answer, look at all the possible answer choices before making the final selection.

(C) Answer: Finally, pick your final answer.

Note: Read each question with the intention of answering the question without looking at the alternate answer choices that follow. Cover the answer choices with your hand or a piece of paper and try to answer the question.

EZ STEP-BY-STEP METHOD: Apply the following steps to think of an answer without looking at the answer choices:

STEP 1: First, try to anticipate or think of an answer before you even look at the answer choices.

STEP 2: Then, check to see if your answer is listed as one of the choices. This can lead to one of the following two scenarios:

> **(A) First Case Scenario:** If the answer that you anticipated happens to be one of the answer choices, or at least happens to very closely match your answer – more than likely, that should be the correct answer, unless you fell into some trap. However, don't just immediately pick that answer choice or assume that is indeed the correct answer. Even if the answer that you formulated happens to be one on the answer choices, you should still always carefully read and consider all the other answer choices before you select your final choice. There may be an even better answer choice farther down the list. The best answer could be the last choice. Frequently, one choice may seem to be the right one until you consider some of the other choices, and you may then realize that the other one is more precise or appropriate. Sometimes, two answers may seem correct, but one may be slightly better than the other. Therefore, read and consider all answer choices before you make your final call.

> **(B) Second Case Scenario:** If the answer that you anticipated does not happen to be one of the answer choices, or does not even come close to any of the given answer choices – you obviously have made some mistake. Go back, read the question again, and try to answer it again, this time probably with a different approach.
> **(i)** If you are not able to find an answer, at least estimate an answer before looking at the answer choices.
> **(ii)** If you still don't get an answer that is listed, read the choices to see which one most closely corresponds to what you think is the correct answer.

ADVANTAGES OF THIS METHOD:

This method often proves to be a better method of finding the correct answer instead of finding the correct answer from the answer choices for the following reasons:

- It will increase your concentration level and improve your memory.
- It will help prevent confusion created by the distracters, which are normally there to confuse or trick you and you'll be much less likely to fall into one of these pre-fabricated traps – the test makers love to bait you with tempting incorrect answer choices.
- It will also boost your confidence and morale since you were able to find the correct answer without the help of the answer choices.
- In most cases, there is a very high likelihood that you will be able to formulate an answer that is identical or at least something very close to one of the answer choices on the test, without the help of the answer choices.

Thinking of an answer before looking at the answer choices reduces the distraction of incorrect answer choices: You must remember that part of the test maker's job is to come up with 3-4 incorrect answer choices for each correct answer. An intelligent test maker will always try to make up those 3-4 incorrect answer choices in a manner that they all look to be pretty good and very close to the correct answer, in order to distract you from the correct answer. This is why these incorrect answer choices are called "distracters." Normally, the test maker tries to make these distracters by including some true element in it, but at the same time they throw in some false element that makes the whole answer choice faulty or wrong. In other words, all the answer choices contain some element of truth which makes them tempting.

Therefore, if you are answering the question without even looking at the answer choices, you already know the answer you should be looking for, and you will not be easily distracted by incorrect answers which may appear to be good. By doing this, you are able to defeat the whole purpose behind these so called distracters, because there is nothing to distract you. This is what we call – giving the test makers their own medicine.

Note for Math Sections: Math questions are more objective. In this case, there are fewer chances of making a mistake because you are generally asked to find the correct answer and not the best answer.

Note for Verbal Sections: Verbal questions are more subjective. Before you look at the choices, think of an answer that makes sense, but don't think that is the correct answer. Always read all the choices in the verbal sections before making your final choice. In the verbal section, you are often looking for the best choice, and that may not necessarily be the correct choice. You may read one of the choices and think that it sounds good, and you may think that you have found the correct answer, but do not automatically assume that it is the correct answer. Do not jump to conclusions too soon. Even if you think you have found the correct answer, you should still read all the other choices. You may be surprised to find that there might be another choice which may even sound better than what you had originally considered. Therefore, on the verbal section, always read all the answer choices before making your final choice.

7.4: THINGS TO REMEMBER WHILE CHANGING ANSWERS:

Change your answers if you are sure; do not change your answers because of any last minute hunch, whim, confusion, or fear: Suddenly you may start thinking that you have selected the incorrect answer choice on a certain question. Should you go with your original answer or change it to another one? Whether you should change your answers or not is an age old controversial subject in test-taking. Research and studies have shown that changes from choosing an incorrect answer to choosing a correct answer outnumber changes that go from choosing a correct answer to choosing an incorrect answer by a sizeable margin of approximately three to one. There are also other researches and studies done that are contradictory to this. Results are mixed, different scholars have different beliefs. Some people think that changing answers can be harmful and will not improve your score and vice versa. We think that these are all myths generated by people and generally attributable to their different experiences and beliefs.

So, what should you do? We suggest you believe neither one of these studies or beliefs, and follow the strategy given below for the most effective use to overcome the confusion surrounding "when" and "if" you should change your first response. There's no easy standard advice that will suit every test-taker under every situation. What you should do depends upon a variety of variables, such as the method you used to answer the question, prior experiences, etc. Before you even decide to change an answer, reason how you approached the question that lead to your first answer. Give some credit to the reasons why you now believe that your first answer may be incorrect and another answer may be a better one. Don't instinctively or impulsively follow some rule without a good reason. Make an intelligent decision based on what you think is now the best way to answer the question.

WHEN TO CHANGE YOUR ANSWERS:

Don't be afraid to change an answer if you are absolutely certain that you had answered it incorrectly. You must also feel confident and strongly about your change of answer. You should only change your answer if you are 100% sure that the first answer you had picked was wrong, you have a strong logical reason to do so, and if you think you actually made a mistake. It would be a very ineffective test-taking strategy to initially hurry through the entire test with the intention or the thought of going back to most of the questions in order to give them a second thought and change your answers. You should instead adopt a systematic approach and make every possible effort to make sure that your first answer is as accurate as possible. Don't change your answers unless you are sure of the correction.

If you return to a question that you have already answered due to extra time, doubt, or any other reason, you should definitely change your answer in any of the following circumstances:
- If you realize you had actually made a mistake.
- If re-reading reveals that you had originally misread, misunderstood, or misinterpreted the question.
- If re-reading suggests that your original reasoning or memory was faulty.
- If you realize that your previous approach to answering the question was faulty.
- If you just remembered some previously learned information.
- If you have developed some new insight from another question.
- If you encountered information elsewhere in the test which indicates with certainty that your first choice is incorrect, or that leads you to the correct answer to an earlier question.
- If you realize you have mis-keyed an answer, that is, you intended to mark a particular answer choice and you inadvertently marked a different choice.

Note: If you do decide to change your answer, always make sure that you completely erase the first mark you had made on the answer sheet and mark the new answer clearly.

WHEN NOT TO CHANGE YOUR ANSWERS:

We suggest that you don't change your answer unless you have a very strong logical reason to do so and you are completely confident. Resist the temptation to change an answer unless you are absolutely certain it's wrong.

Do Not Second Guess: If you are guessing on the question, the answer which comes to mind first is often correct. Reviewing your answer choices with an anxious mind and changing your answers when you are not certain can do more harm than good. Normally, your first guess, intuition, or hunch is more likely to be correct than your subsequent guesses, so be sure to have a sound and logical reason for changing your answer. Do not "second-guess" yourself and change your original answer just for the sake of it. The answer which comes first to your mind is more likely to be correct, and changing your answer on a last-minute hunch, whim, confusion, or fear mostly leads to selecting an incorrect answer choice. Moreover, by the time you have gone through the test once and come back to a question for the second time, you will be tired and exhausted, and any guesses or decisions that you make at that time are likely to be less accurate than the ones you originally made when you answered that question previously. In addition, you would have had more time in hand to think and get the answer while you attempted the question for the first time than the second time. Remember, your first response comes from some undisclosed location in your memory bank even if it was a calculated guess.

BOTTOM LINE:

The bottom line is that you should change your answer only because you really think you made an actual error, and not because of any last minute hunch, whim, confusion, or fear. If you know you actually made an error, change your first answer. If you know it was just a guess, keep your first impression.

7.5: TEST ANSWERING TIPS:

WHEN TWO OR MORE ANSWER CHOICES LOOK GOOD:

Frequently, you may come across a difficult situation when two or more answer choices look apparently good and it's hard for you to choose one of them. Remember, there must be only one correct answer to each question. Also, check to see if one of them answers the question more precisely and accurately than the others. Try to apply some of the following points:

- Try to find differences between those two or more answer choices that look good to you, and eventually those differences will make one of them correct and others wrong.
- If two alternatives seem correct, compare them for their differences, and then refer to the stem to find your best answer.
- One of the choices may not completely address the question, meaning, it may only be partly correct or is too narrow or broad.
- One of the choices may reflect a common misconception or misunderstanding, instead of what is actually true or can be proven. Answers like these will probably be wrong.

WHEN ALL THE ANSWER CHOICES LOOK BAD:

You may also encounter a difficult situation when all the answer choices look bad. Remember, there is always one correct answer to each question, unless one of the answer choices has a special phrase "none of the above" or "not enough information given."

CORRECT ANSWER VS. BEST ANSWER:

MULTIPLE CHOICE MEANS MULTIPLE-CONFUSION:

Multiple choice questions sometimes bring with them multiple confusions. In fact, multiple choice questions are designed to be tricky and confusing.

Following are the two types of multiple choice questions that have multiple answer choices available:

(A) With only one "correct" answer choice.

Correct Answer: means there is only one correct answer choice, like in the math section.

(B) With only one "best" answer choice.

Best Answer: means there may be more than one correct answer or there may not be a completely correct answer, but there is only one best possible answer choice which is more correct than other choices, like in the verbal section.

Note: Correct answer and best answer are two different things and you must know the difference between the two.

HOW TO CHOOSE THE CORRECT ANSWER:

Choosing the correct answer is not that difficult, and the difference between the right and the wrong answer choices is fairly prominent. There should be less confusion when you are asked to choose the correct answer since you already know that there is only one correct answer and the rest are all incorrect answer choices. But, at the same time, make sure you understand the question and your answer is accurate so that it matches one, and only one, of the possible answer choices.

HOW TO CHOOSE THE BEST ANSWER:

Recognizing the best answer can sometimes be tricky and confusing since there is no one correct answer, and the differences among the answer choices are not as diverse or prominent as black and white. In this case, more than one of the possible answers may be "arguably correct," and the "best" answer is among those "potentially correct" ones. It may sometimes happen that the most adequate, correct and technically the most complete answer may not even happen to be one of the answer choices to a question. It is sometimes difficult for test makers to include an answer choice that is the ideal answer to the question asked. The main reason is that an answer choice which includes all the correct elements may then become awfully long. Therefore, some of the answer choices may only be partially correct, and one of them may be slightly better than others and that makes that answer choice to be a better one. Your job is to choose the best possible choice among those partially correct answer choices. The best way to answer such types of questions is by using the process of elimination technique and eliminating all the answer choices that are definitely wrong or very seriously incomplete. Next, compare the remaining answer choices. For more details, look at the process of elimination section discussed later in this book.

GRADING SYSTEM:

A more objective approach to finding the best answer is by using the grading system.

STEP 1: First, try to grade the alternative answer choices from a scale of 1 to 5, where 1 indicates a completely incorrect answer and 5 indicates a completely correct answer choice.

STEP 2: Next, after eliminating completely incorrect answer choices, you may be left with two remaining answer choices that look equally good.

    (A) You should then make fine distinctions while evaluating the remaining answer choices and choose the answer that you think is at least a slightly better answer.

    (B) In most cases, you should be only left with one answer choice, which will be your best answer to the question.

FOR QUESTIONS THAT HAVE "ALL OF THE ABOVE" AS AN ANSWER CHOICE:

Choose: If you are sure that more than one of the options is definitely correct – you should choose the option "all of the above."

Eliminate: If you are sure that at least one of the options is definitely incorrect – you should eliminate the option "all of the above", and choose from the remaining answer choices.

FOR QUESTIONS THAT HAVE "NONE OF THE ABOVE" AS AN ANSWER CHOICE:

Choose: If you are sure that all of the options are definitely incorrect – you should choose the option "none of the above."

Eliminate: If you are sure that at least one of the options is correct – you should eliminate the option "none of the above", and choose from the remaining answer choices.

FOR QUESTIONS THAT HAVE "IT CANNOT BE SOLVED" OR "NOT ENOUGH INFORMATION GIVEN" AS AN ANSWER CHOICE:

Choose: If you are sure that there is not enough information in the question in order to solve it – you should choose this option.

Eliminate: If you are sure that there is enough information in the question in order to solve it – you should eliminate this option.

PART 8.0: PACING STRATEGY:

TABLE OF CONTENTS:

THIS PAGE HAS BEEN INTENTIONALLY LEFT BLANK.

8.1: ABOUT PACING STRATEGY:

Your test has a fixed number of questions which must be answered within a specific and limited amount of time. That's why pacing is such an important aspect of taking any time-bound standardized test. Pacing strategy is based on the idea that each question on the test requires a certain amount of time to read and answer. You should also plan and sense your time, and accordingly pace yourself, in order to complete the test in the given amount of time. If you were given unlimited time to answer the given questions, pacing would not even be an issue. But the fact of the matter is that all standardized tests have limited test time. You should have one clear objective in mind – to score the maximum points you can – it's that simple. Our books will help you do just that. Therefore, it's very important to pace yourself while taking the test and the goal of pacing strategy is that you answer all the questions to the best of your abilities within the allotted time.

DON'T RUSH OR GET BOGGED DOWN:
Speed with accuracy – the name of the game is increasing the speed of your work without sacrificing accuracy.

(A) **Don't Rush:** While pacing yourself, do not rush through the question, but don't spend excessive time on any one question either. If you rush through the questions, you may feel out of control or you may make careless errors where you may end up answering even the easier questions incorrectly. Don't let your fear about the time stand in the way of your work. Answering one question correctly is better than hurrying to answer three questions and answering all of them incorrectly. Give each question your absolute best and move on so that you can minimize guessing and have enough time to consider each test question in a section.

(B) **Don't Get Bogged Down:** Work as carefully as possible, but you should not get bogged down or stumped on any one question. If you face a tough, time-consuming question and you can't answer it within a reasonable amount of time, or you aren't sure about how to answer it, or don't know where to even begin – the best policy is to pace yourself by using your time wisely by being aware of the number of questions and time remaining. You may end up spending too much time on one difficult baffling question, leaving insufficient time to answer the easy questions by running out of time. By spending too much time on any one question, you may be giving up the opportunity to answer the other questions correctly. So you could spend a lot of time on one difficult question and still not be able to answer it correctly, when you could have probably spent that same time answering 5-7 easy questions correctly, and quite easily. Doing this will get your mental process and concentration ready for more difficult questions. Remember, higher scores will usually result from trying all questions. Don't cloud your mind by lingering for too long over any one question. Don't let it discourage you or affect your attitude and steal your valuable time. There's no point of honor at stake here, but there are points on the line waiting for you to grab them. Yes, letting go of a tough question may not be an easy job for everyone. It's human nature, we all want to ace through a test and answer every question as it comes to us. But that mindset doesn't work here. If you try to plow your shoes too hard on a tough question, repudiating to move on until you get it right, you're letting your test ego get in the way of your test score. Therefore, use your time wisely and never get bogged down on any one question.

PACING FOR WRITING SECTION:
Pacing for the Writing section would depend upon each individual's writing style. We suggest that before you start writing your response, you should think about the essay and write bullet points on your scratch paper or test booklet. Next, you should start writing your response while keeping in mind that you need to minimize any additions, deletions, or corrections. Finally, keep few minutes towards the end for proof reading and many any corrections.

8.2: TIME MANAGEMENT:

Whenever you have limited means to meet your end, you have to often resort to budgeting. For instance, when you have a fixed income, you have to budget your money to various heads so that you can meet all your expenses. Likewise, the same situation applies in taking a test. Here, your fixed income is the fixed amount of time, and your expenses are the questions. In other words, you have a fixed amount of time in which you have to finish all the questions. The major difference between budgeting your income and test time is if you go over your budget, you can borrow from a bank or credit card, but unfortunately, there are no such options available while taking a test. Here, you have to learn to live within your means, and you've got to finish answering the questions in the fixed allotted time, not a second above that. Therefore, it is almost inevitable to budget your test time to ensure that you finish answering all the questions in the allotted time. It is of utmost importance that you keep a close track of your time.

SET THE MOMENTUM AND KEEP MOVING:

Try to set the momentum by working quickly through each question of each section at an even and steady pace. Keep moving and don't stop, but don't go too fast where you end up making silly and careless mistakes, and don't go too slow, so that you fall short of time.

TIME BUDGETING:

You have worked hard in preparing for this challenging test, and now you want to do your best on it. The last thing you want to happen to you is to be out of time and not be able to answer all the questions. Hence, it's critical that you pace yourself, so this doesn't happen to you. Determine a pace which will ensure completing the whole test in time. Make use of the general pacing guidelines explained in this section to your advantage.

Time is of the Essence: You only have a limited amount of time for each section, so pace yourself carefully. Start working as soon as the test time begins and keep working until the last minute of the test period. Time is of the essence, so don't waste even a single second. Use a stop-watch or a clock to better pace yourself.

Rate of Time per Question: It is important to plan and divide your allotted time appropriately in advance for each test question. Most books advise you to divide the total number of questions by the total number of minutes, and they suggest that's how long you should plan to spend on each question. We think this is the most erroneous advice when it comes to pacing. Discrimination is usually not the best policy, but not when it comes to pacing. Not all questions are of the same level of complexity and difficulty, and you shouldn't treat all the questions with equal dignity and spend an equal amount of time on each one of them. While setting up a time-schedule, remember that not all the questions are equally time-consuming. Some questions take less time than others, and some questions take more time than others. Generally, for most people, it takes more time to answer the difficult questions than it does to answer the easy ones. You need to go swiftly through the easy questions and decelerate a bit while going through the difficult ones. For instance, if there are 60 questions in a section and you have 60 minutes to finish them, it does not mean that you should spend 1 minute per question. For instance, a simple arithmetic question or a simple sentence correction question can be answered within 15 – 20 seconds or less, whereas, a complex word problem or a complex reading comprehension question could take 2 minutes or longer to answer. Remember, standardized tests do not test whether you can answer the questions correctly; instead they test whether you can answer the questions correctly in the given amount of time.

What you need to do is to develop a sense of how much time to spend on each question type so that you can better pace yourself and keep a check on the speed at which you are working. You'll know when you're moving too slow and when you need to move a little bit faster. The best way to develop a sense of good timing is by timing yourself while practicing questions in all our different books. This will give you a good idea of how long you will need for each question type during an actual test. You will also be able to find out whether you are answering quickly enough to complete the test section in the allotted time.

Split a Test Section into Groups: You may also want to split the total number of questions into smaller groups and fix a time for each group. For instance, if you have a total of 50 questions to answer in 60 minutes, consider it as either two groups of 25 questions at 30 minutes for each group, or five groups of 10 questions at 12 minutes for each group. It's important that you keep track of your progress as you finish each group. If you are on schedule, you are doing great, if not, you'll need to pick up your pace. You must also set aside a few minutes at the end of each section for a quick review of your work.

Time Schedule: Plan your time and set up a time schedule for progress throughout each test section. Budget enough time for each question type so that you can complete the test without having to rush at the end of each section. Decide in advance, after how much time you should be one-quarter way through and/or half-way way through of each test section. Try to stick to that time plan and finish the test in the allotted time. If you are halfway through the test and you have answered half of the questions, it may not necessarily mean that you are in the proper timeframe since the majority of the questions that you have already answered may be the easy ones – so, remember to factor this in while checking your progress against the remaining time. Periodically, check your progress against the time-schedule that you had set in advance throughout the test so that you know when you are one-quarter and/or half way through the time allotted for the section. If you are behind your time-schedule, you need to speed up and if you are ahead of your time schedule, you need to slow down a little.

Towards the End of a Section: You also need to change your pacing strategy as you move through a test section. Your pace should change slightly when you are at the beginning of a section than when you are at the middle or when you are approaching the end of a section. If you are at the middle of a section and you find that more than half of the questions remain unanswered, you know that you need to accelerate your pace. If you only have a few minutes remaining and too many questions to answer, you know that you need to switch to the overdrive mode. You should keep track of your time every minute during the last five minutes of the test time period. Manage your time properly so that you have sufficient time to answer all the questions, and finish the test on time.

You'll Have Sufficient Time: The test has been designed so that most people taking it are able to finish each individual test section in time. Many people will even have time to go back and check their work. So, don't worry unnecessarily, you will have enough time to complete all the questions in time. All you need to do is to use all the available time and do your very best on the test. At the same time, the test you are taking is designed to challenge all types of test-takers. So, all test-takers, regardless of their intelligence level, must expect to find some difficult and challenging questions. Do not allow yourself to get flustered by one difficult question to a point that it completely throws off your performance on the rest of the section. A rough time with one nasty question will not mess up your score; however, lingering or cribbing over it will definitely throw you off-track.

THIS PAGE HAS BEEN INTENTIONALLY LEFT BLANK.

PART 9.0: GUESSING WITH PROCESS OF ELIMINATION:

TABLE OF CONTENTS:

THIS PAGE HAS BEEN INTENTIONALLY LEFT BLANK.

9.1: GUESSING:

On multiple choice questions, the answers are right in front of you – you just have to find them. This makes the multiple choice questions vulnerable in several different ways to finding an answer, such as guessing techniques. On multiple choice questions, first look for the best answer rather than trying to guess. If you are unable to identify the best choice, only then should you guess. Improve the odds of getting the correct answer while guessing by using the process of elimination (PoE) to make educated guesses.

SHOULD YOU GUESS?

If you don't know the answer to a question, should you guess or not on a test is an age old controversial subject. If you ask this question to different people for their opinion, you are bound to get conflicting answers. In general, our advice is: for questions you are unsure how to answer directly, guessing is a good idea, but only if you have an effective guessing strategy. Understanding our guessing strategy will help you make the best use of guessing while taking a multiple choice test.

GUESSING IS SOMETIMES INEVITABLE:

The fact is that everyone guesses at some point or the other, for one reason or another. Yes, even some of the smartest test-takers guess sometimes. Whether it is because you have hit a question that totally flabbergasts you or you are running short of time, you will find that you have to guess occasionally, if not frequently.

GUESSING MAKES SENSE:

Every question is worth exactly the same amount of one point. You do not get more credit for a correct answer to the hardest question than you do for the easiest one. With each correct answer you gain one point. If you leave the answer blank, you get no point. If your answer is wrong, you only lose a fraction of a point. Therefore, it makes sense to guess using an effective guessing strategy.

PENALTY FOR INCORRECT ANSWERS (NEGATIVE MARKING):

There is never a penalty for guessing on any test; however, there may be a penalty for guessing the incorrect answer.

(A) **If there is No Penalty for Incorrect Answers:** When there is no penalty for guessing, always make the best use of guessing. Only your correct answers are used to determine your score. Your incorrect answers don't have any negative effect on your final score. For every correct answer, you get one point. For every incorrect answer, you don't get any points and you don't lose any points. Since, there is no negative marking for an incorrect answer, it always pays to guess. Of course, while guessing, you should try to use the process of elimination technique to its maximum. But even if you don't have a clue about a question, you should still guess and never leave any questions unmarked. You never know, as you might just get lucky, and there is nothing to lose. If there are no chances of losing, but there are some chances of winning, you should definitely try your luck.

(B) **If there is a Penalty for Incorrect Answers:** When there is a penalty for guessing, only indulge in educated guessing, and stay far away from random guessing. Even if you lose points for guessing incorrect answers, it may still make some sense to make educated guesses. The fractional points you lose for guessing incorrect answers can be offset by the points you might earn by accidentally guessing the correct answers. On the other hand, if you guess at random on many questions, the points you lose on incorrect guesses could cancel out the points you gain from correct guesses. In this case, your net gain will not be zero, you'll be losing some very precious time by guessing these questions, which you could have used to answer the questions you know or to recheck your answers. Hence, be careful while guessing if there is a penalty for each incorrect answer. Don't random guess if you are going to be penalized for guessing and if you don't have any basis for your guess.

9.2: PROCESS OF ELIMINATION:

Process of elimination is a process which lets you eliminate one or more incorrect answer choices. The core idea behind using the process of elimination technique to its maximum and then making an educated and intelligent guess is to be able to eliminate all but one correct answer choice. Obviously, that would be the perfect scenario. In a partially perfect scenario, you should at least be able to eliminate one or more possible answer choices, and then make an educated guess from the remaining ones. Hence, if you are able to eliminate some of the answer choices, guessing can prove to be a profitable proposition.

PROCESS OF ELIMINATION + EDUCATED GUESSING = MAKES SENSE!

DON'T OMIT QUESTIONS THAT YOU ARE NOT SURE HOW TO ANSWER:
There will always be a few questions that you are not sure how to answer or have absolutely no idea how to answer. Do not omit these questions. By omitting these questions, you may be losing some valuable points. With proper use of our guessing strategy, and with the effective use of the process of elimination, you can correctly answer a lot of questions that you may not otherwise know how to answer.

SOMETIMES IT'S EASIER TO FIND THE INCORRECT ANSWER THAN THE CORRECT ONE:
If you don't know how to find the correct answer to a question, try to eliminate the wrong ones. It is sometimes easier to find the incorrect answers than the correct answer. Occasionally, you will be surprised that on some questions, you can eliminate all the answer choices until you only have one correct answer choice left. In other words, eliminating incorrect answer choices can help you think your way through, and eventually lead you to the correct answer. On most of the questions, you should be able to eliminate one or more of the answer choices. Therefore, first eliminate as many answer choices as you can, and then make your best guess from among the remaining answer choices.

GUESS VS. EDUCATED & INTELLIGENT GUESS:
There is a lucid difference between random and intelligent guessing. If you are not sure of an answer, or you are absolutely clueless, it is always recommended that you make an educated and intelligent guess in the multiple choice questions. It is better to first use the process of elimination to the maximum, try to eliminate one or more choices, and then compare the remaining answer choices to determine the differences and make an educated guess from the remaining ones. As soon as you start eliminating incorrect answer choices, you have entered the zone of intelligent guessing where your chances of selecting the correct answer increase with each choice you eliminate. For almost all the questions, you should be able to eliminate at least a few answer choices. So, don't just make a guess, make an educated and intelligent guess. Smart guessing with PoE can significantly minimize the risk of guessing the wrong answers and maximize the odds of picking the ones.

WILD - BLIND - RANDOM GUESSING:
If you are not sure of an answer, it is not recommended that you make a wild, blind, or random guess. Random guessing probably will not improve your test score. In fact, it may result in lowering your test score. Therefore, make an educated and intelligent guess, and stay away from random guessing. Random guessing should be used only as a last resort.

ELIMINATE ABSOLUTELY ABSURD & OBVIOUSLY INCORRECT ANSWER CHOICES:
Absolutely absurd and obviously incorrect answer choices can never be the correct answer choice. Use the process of elimination, narrow down your choices by trying to eliminate all the absolutely absurd and obviously incorrect answer choices. In most questions, at least one or more answer choices will be absolutely absurd or obviously incorrect, and you should be able to eliminate them easily. For instance, if a question is asking for the area of a cube, the answer has to be in square units – you can easily eliminate any answer choice that is not in square units.

CHANCES OF SUCCESS WHILE GUESSING & USING PROCESS OF ELIMINATION:
The probability of selecting the correct answer by random guessing is 1 out of 5, or 20%, which is quite low. However, you can increase your chances of getting the correct answer by guessing and using the process of elimination. The more answer choices you are able to eliminate, the greater are your chances of choosing the correct answer. With each answer choice you eliminate, you increase your chances of guessing correctly. If you can eliminate even one answer, you increase your chances of getting a question correct. Making a decision between two choices is easier than deciding among three, four, or five choices. Therefore, try to eliminate as many choices as you can before making a guess.

Always remember, educated and intelligent guessing can significantly increase your scores. By learning our exclusive EZ strategies given in this and our other books, you can eliminate incorrect answer choices on almost all the questions, even when you have no idea about the actual correct answer. By eliminating the incorrect answer choices, you are creating a guessing advantage and a pathway to the correct answer.

TABLE OF PROBABILITY OF GETTING THE CORRECT ANSWER WHILE GUESSING WITH PoE:

Refer to the following table to see your chances or the probability of getting the correct answer while guessing and using the process of elimination:

- If you are able to eliminate "zero" answer choices ⇒ You have a 20% chance of guessing the correct answer.
- If you are able to eliminate "one" answer choice ⇒ You have a 25% chance of guessing the correct answer.
- If you are able to eliminate "two" answer choices ⇒ You have a 33.33% chance of guessing the correct answer.
- If you are able to eliminate "three" answer choices ⇒ You have a 50% chance of guessing the correct answer.
- If you are able to eliminate "four" answer choices ⇒ You have a 100% chance of guessing the correct answer.
- If you are able to eliminate "all" answer choices ⇒ You have made a mistake, go back, and start over again!

APPLY THE FOLLOWING LABELING SYSTEM FOR MOST EFFECTIVE USE OF PoE:

Check Mark: "✓"   ⇒ Correct Answer Choice.
Indicates you have successfully been able to eliminate all the answer choices but this one, and therefore, this is the correct answer.

Double Check Mark: "✓✓"   ⇒ Double Checked Correct Answer.
Indicates you have successfully been able to eliminate all the answer choices but this one, and you have double checked all the answer choices again.

Cross Mark: "✗"   ⇒ Incorrect Answer Choice & Not Possible.
Indicates you have decided to eliminate this answer choice from consideration.

Single Question Mark: "?"   ⇒ Possible & Probable.
Indicates you are not yet sure whether to eliminate this answer choice from consideration.

Double Question Mark: "??"   ⇒ Not Likely, but still Possible.
Indicates you are quite sure but not yet completely sure whether to eliminate this answer choice from consideration.

Blank Mark/Unmarked: "   "   ⇒ Not Yet Read.
Indicates you have not yet read this answer choice.

PROCESS OF ELIMINATION (PoE) STRATEGY:

FROM POSSIBILITY TO PROBABILITY TO GETTING THE CORRECT ANSWER:

The idea behind using process of elimination is to start from possibilities to probabilities in finding the correct answer:

STEP 1: First, review all the "possible" answer choices.

STEP 2: Then, eliminate the answer choices that are "impossible".

STEP 3: Then, reconsider the remaining "probable" answer choices.

STEP 4: Then, again eliminate the answer choices that you now think are "impossible".

Repeat this process until you are able to eliminate all but one of the answer choices.
(A) If only one answer choice is left, that is your correct answer.
(B) If more than one answer choice is left, make an educated and intelligent guess.

EZ-STEP-BY-STEP METHOD: Use the Following Steps to Apply Process of Elimination:

STEP 1: REVIEW ALL POSSIBLE ANSWER CHOICES: One-by-one, review all the possible answer choices:
     (A) Cross-Out (X) Obviously Incorrect Answer Choices: As soon as you eliminate an answer choice from considering it to be one of the possible answer choices ⇒ make sure to cross it out by putting a big cross (X) mark on the letter of that answer choice in your question booklet (or scratch paper) so you know that it is not one of the possible answer choices.
     (B) Put a Question Mark (?) for Answer Choices Still under Consideration: If you are not yet sure about an answer choice and you are still considering it to be one of the possible and probable answer choices ⇒

make sure to put a question (?) mark next to the letter of that answer choice in your question booklet (or scratch paper) so you know that it is still one of the probable answer choices, and you can come back to it for re-consideration.

STEP 2: REVIEW ALL PROBABLE ANSWER CHOICES: Go back to the answer choices with a question-mark and try to eliminate as many as you can.

(A) **You May Get The Obvious Correct Answer:** If you are able to eliminate all but one of the probable answer choices, then that answer choice which has not been eliminated should be your correct answer. You have successfully been able to reach a point where the process of elimination has led you to the correct answer choice.

(B) **You May Have To Make An Educated And Intelligent Guess:** If you are not able to eliminate all but one of the probable answer choices, meaning, if you still have more than one answer choice that you have not been able to eliminate, you have no other choice but to make an educated and intelligent guess from the remaining probable answer choices.

Note: If you realize that you eliminated all answer choices, obviously you have made a mistake – go back and start over.

ADVANTAGES OF OUR PROCESS OF ELIMINATION STRATEGY:

- It helps in avoiding reconsidering answer choices that you have already eliminated.
- It helps in narrowing down the possible answer choices.
- It also makes it possible to answer a question which you are not sure about and/or do not know how to answer at all, with the highest chances of getting it correct.
- It can also sometimes lead you to the correct answer if you are able to eliminate four of the five answer choices.

9.3: OTHER GUESSING SUGGESTIONS:

If everything else fails and you have to guess an answer, only then consider the following suggestions:

SIMILAR ANSWER CHOICES: (LOOK ALIKE OPTIONS)

(A) **If two or more answer choices are "exactly" similar:** choose neither one of them since there is only one correct answer. Eliminate choices that basically mean the same thing, and thus cancel each other out.

(B) **If two options are "extremely" similar, but not "exactly" similar, except for one or two words:** choose one of them, since it is very likely that one of them is the correct answer, the test maker was probably trying to throw in a distracter that was very close to the correct answer.

OPPOSITE ANSWER CHOICES: (ECHO OPTIONS)

If two answer choices are "completely" opposite of each other, choose one of them since it is very likely that one of them is the correct answer.

ELIMINATE EXTREME NUMBER CHOICES: CHOOSE ONE OF THE MIDDLE VALUES:

Avoid extremes, prefer middle range answer choices. If two answers seem extreme, they should be eliminated and a guess should be made from the remaining ones. For instance, if 1, 5, 7, 9, 15 are the possible answer choices, eliminate the high and low, 1 and 15, and choose from the middle range numbers, 5, 7, and 9.

FAMILIAR ANSWER CHOICES AND UNFAMILIAR ANSWER CHOICES:

Guessing can be used when one of the answer choices sounds familiar. When an answer choice sounds familiar, it may trigger some form of recall that involves material you have previously covered. So, that familiar choice may be the correct answer due to information deep in your long-term memory. Select that choice over an unknown or unfamiliar answer choice.

9.4: HOW TO GUESS IF YOU ARE CLUELESS:

If you don't know how to answer a question and do not have a clue to even make an educated guess, there is no other way to answer the question but to make a random guess. However, don't just close your eyes and pick an answer choice. A better way to improve your odds would be if you include some sense into this guessing game. Try to always rationalize your answer. You don't always need a perfect reason to prefer one answer choice over another. Sometimes, an intelligent guess can be based purely on a hunch or an intuition, such as, something you may already know but are not able to consciously identify it. You may not be able to find a logical reasoning phenomenon but you can make use of the following advice in such a case:

- Use your common sense to choose an answer to the question, which may or may not lead you to the correct answer.
- Use the power of your hunch or whim.

LENGTH OF AN ANSWER CHOICE:

When guessing an answer, pick the longest answer – it is relatively easier for the test makers to write short incorrect answers than long ones. But be careful, the correct answer has to be precise, to the point, and not overly wordy. The length of the choices is sometimes a clue. If one answer is unusually long or short, it is usually the correct answer. Select the answers that are longer, complete, and more descriptive. Longer answers stand out and contain more details and are often correct. Shorter answers are created quickly, and are often wrong. Descriptive details will be given to help you identify the truth.

MYTHS ABOUT GUESSING:

You've probably heard many advices about how to answer questions when you don't know the correct answer. Some of the most common advices are listed below:

- When in doubt, select answer choice C.
- When in doubt, select the longest (or shortest) alternatives.
- If NONE OF THE ABOVE (or a similar response) is among the answer choices, select it.

There may be some truth to these advices but there is no scientific proof to prove their validity. You must realize that the test makers are aware of these suggestions and they take them into account while designing test questions and multiple choices in order to make these advices ineffective. Moreover, you are going to take a test to prove your intelligence, not trying your luck by picking numbers for the lottery. Hence, our advice is to eliminate any possible answer choices based on your knowledge and then make your best guess.

PART 10.0: PAPER-BASED TEST FORMAT STRATEGIES:

TABLE OF CONTENTS:

THIS PAGE HAS BEEN INTENTIONALLY LEFT BLANK.

10.1: IMPORTANT TIPS FOR PAPER-BASED TEST FORMAT:

Important Note: Following strategies are only applicable if you are taking a paper-based version of the test. These strategies do not apply to the computer-adaptive format. Note that if you are in a foreign country, a military base, a remote location, or there are some other extreme circumstances, you may have to take the paper-based version of the test. Hence, apply the strategies given in this chapter only if you are taking the paper-based version of the test.

MAKE SURE YOU HAVE THE COMPLETE TEST AND ANSWER SHEETS:
Right after you have been given your test – quickly check to make sure that you have all the pages and sections in the test booklet and the corresponding answer sheet. In most cases, you will be told the number of pages in your test booklet. If any page is missing, or if it has some printing problem due to which the text is skewed, distorted, or not legible, immediately raise your hand and inform the test proctor.

SCAN/BROWSE THROUGH THE ENTIRE TEST:
The first step after you are handed over the test is to scan through the whole test for a few seconds and analyze it before beginning to answer the questions. By doing this, you will get a feel of what's on the test. This will also give you an overview of the test and you can accordingly strategize yourself and plan how you should attack the test. This process should not take more than a few seconds of your test time.

BREAK EACH SECTION INTO SUB-SECTIONS:
Instead of looking at each section as one big test, it may be helpful to divide each section into sub-sections based on types of questions. For instance, you can first divide the whole math section into algebra, geometry, and word problems, and then tackle each sub-section in the order in which you want.

MARK KEY WORDS IN QUESTIONS:
Underlining or circling key words in each question is an effective test-taking strategy to focus on the central point, which is what's being asked and not what you thought is being asked, and it also minimizes careless mistakes. Frequently, you may be misled or fall into a trap because you may have overlooked a key word in the question. Also, make sure that you answer what is asked, not what you think is being asked. Therefore, always underline or circle key words in each question to make sure that you are not missing any key information given in the question, and you are able to focus on what is being asked, and not fall into any traps. Remember, you are allowed to mark and write anything you wish on your test booklet (for paper-based tests) or scratch paper (for computer-based tests), so take advantage of this opportunity.

DON'T MISS OUT ON A PAGE OF QUESTIONS:
It is possible that out of carelessness, you forget to turn over the page and miss out on a page full of questions. Be very careful, and make sure you keep going until you see "this is the end of the test", and answer all the questions.

YOU DON'T HAVE TO ANSWER EVERY QUESTION CORRECTLY TO DO WELL:
Always remember that you don't have to answer every question (correctly) to do well. It is possible to omit or get a few questions wrong and still be able to get a reasonably good score. For paper-based tests, you may be able to do better if you skip a few questions since that will give you more time per question and you can use your time wisely. It is always better to answer fewer questions and get most of them correct instead of trying to attempt all the questions and get most of them incorrect. This technique can dramatically improve your score. As per research and studies, one can get a much higher score by not trying to answer every question. Therefore, based on your target score, plan in advance how many questions you should attempt and how many you can afford to omit.

ANSWER ONE QUESTION AT A TIME:
You should answer one question at a time and not let any other question affect your performance on the particular question that you are tackling. Try to give all your energy and concentration to the question you are attempting, and don't think about any other question that you saw previously or may be able to see on the same page.

10.2: ANSWER EVERY QUESTION:

TRY TO ANSWER EVERY QUESTION YOU ATTEMPT:

It is recommended that you answer every question you attempt. If you attempt a question and you are unable to get the correct answer, you will at least have a feel about the question, and it is very likely that you would be able to eliminate at least one or more answer choices. Moreover, since you have already invested some of your time into the question, it's worth taking a chance by making an educated guess. Therefore, answer every question you attempt, by first eliminating as many choices as you can, and then make an educated guess.

NEVER LEAVE ANY QUESTION UNMARKED:

You must try to answer all the questions, even if you do not have any idea how to answer some of them or don't have enough time to eliminate any of the options. Specially during the last few minutes of the test section, if you realize that you are not going to be able to finish all the questions on a particular test section on time – then before you are instructed to put your pencil down, simply fill in the answers randomly on the answer sheet for those questions that you didn't have time to answer. You have at least a chance of getting some of them correct. Even the wildest guess has a 20% chance of being correct, but a blank has a 0% chance of being correct. If possible, never leave any question unmarked on the answer sheet. Therefore, try to answer each and every question on the test, even if you have to make a random guess.

Special Instructions for Reading Comprehension Section: Don't leave any reading comprehension question unanswered if you have read the passage. If you have read the passage, it is very likely that you would be able to eliminate one or more answer choices, and hence, by eliminating those choices, you will have a greater chance of getting the correct answer while making an educated guess.

Special Instructions for Math Section: You should be able to eliminate one or more choices in most of the math questions. Mostly, all of the math questions contain at least one or more choices that are completely absurd or obviously incorrect; and hence, by eliminating those choices, you will have a greater chance of getting the correct answer while making an educated guess.

NEVER TURN IN YOUR TEST BEFORE TIME:

You should never turn in your test before the test time is up even if you think you have completed the test, and resist the urge to leave as soon as you have completed the test. If you finish a section before the allotted time, don't sit idle, use the remaining time to review and double check your answers, and make sure you answered all questions, marked the answers at the right spot on the answer sheet, and didn't make silly mistakes. Proofread your writing for spelling, grammar, punctuation, decimal points, etc. Remember that you cannot go to the next section until the proctor tells you to do so.

ALWAYS TRY TO CHECK YOUR WORK:

If you get to the end of one of the individual test sections with several minutes remaining, you may feel tired of juggling boring questions. During this time, you can relax and close your eyes, look around the room and see the tense faces of other people, or you can utilize this time by checking your answers.
Note: You can only work on the current section during the allotted time. If you finish earlier, you can't start working on the next section.
Here are some of the things you can do during these last few remaining minutes:
- See if you inadvertently missed out on any question.
- Check if you have marked your answers cleanly at only one spot for each question at the correct spots on the answer sheet or on the computer.
- If there are too many questions left for you to check, first check those that you feel most uncertain about, and then spend the remaining time on any others that you have time for.
- You may want to take a few minutes to go over your essay. Make sure to correct any mistakes in spelling, grammar, usage, or punctuation. If you see any words that are hard to read, rewrite them legibly so that the scorers can read them easily.

10.3: ORDER OF ANSWERING QUESTIONS:

If you are given a choice to answer the questions in any order you want and hop around the questions within each section, you need to have a plan to answer the questions in a strategic order. It is not usually a good idea to start with question #1 and not stop until you've answered every question in sequence. Like most test-takers, you always have the option to go through the questions from the beginning to the end, or if you happen to be one of those savvy test-takers, you will create your own strategic path.

You can answer the questions in any order, and you don't have to answer the questions in the order in which they are presented to you. You can answer the questions in your strongest subject first and then move on to your weaker areas, or you can answer the questions that you think are less time-consuming first and then move on to the more time-consuming questions. There is no right or wrong way – use the approach that works best for you based on your experience with your prior tests and practice questions.

ALL QUESTIONS ARE WORTH EQUAL POINTS:

All questions, both easy and difficult, are worth equal number of points. The contribution of each correct answer towards your final score or the score value of each correct answer is the same, regardless of the type of question or the level of difficulty of the question. Since each question is worth equal number of points, you should treat each question equally. You should answer the easy questions first, and then spend the remaining time in answering the more difficult ones. But of course, the easy questions will take slightly less time to answer than the more difficult ones. If you get two easy ones correct in the same time as you would have taken to get a hard one correct, you just gained an extra point. Therefore, it is not wise to spend a lot of time on any single question since they all are worth equal number of points. Remember, it's the quantity and not the quality that counts. All questions, no matter how easy or hard they are, or what topic they belong to, will count equally towards your total score. Since you don't get more points for answering hard questions or fewer points for easier ones, rack up as many points as you can.

FIRST ANSWER EASY QUESTIONS, THEN DIFFICULT ONES:

Answer the questions in the strategic order of increasing difficulty. It is common sense that easy questions are easy to answer and difficult questions are difficult to answer. So, it is very important to be aware of the level of difficulty of each question. As the difficulty level increases, it gets harder and harder to answer the more difficult questions. Answer the questions in the order of difficulty, starting from answering the easiest question first to the most difficult question towards the end. Remember, easy and hard are relative terms; what might be easy for one student might be hard for another, and vice versa.

FIRST ANSWER QUESTIONS YOU ARE GOOD AT, THEN OTHERS:

By the time you are ready to take the test, you will have a fairly good idea about the types of questions you are good at. Do those questions first and take advantage of knowing your strengths. By the same token, do the questions that you are not so good at, later. Invest your valuable time in your strengths, not weaknesses. Remember, you will not always be good at only the easy questions; sometimes, you may find yourself good at some of the more difficult questions, and you should do those first. In short, spend the majority of your time on the questions that you have the ability or skills to answer and you are most likely to answer them correctly, and spend any remaining time on trying to answer the other questions. For instance, in the math section, you may be particularly good at answering ratio problems, so do those first; and you may not be so good at answering probability questions, so do those later. For instance, in the verbal section, you may be particularly good at answering the main idea, or tone questions, so do those first; and you may not be so good at answering organization or inference questions, so do those later.

FIRST ANSWER LESS TIME-CONSUMING QUESTIONS, THEN MORE TIME-CONSUMING ONES:

There may be questions that you know how to answer correctly but are very time-consuming – do them after you answer the less-time consuming questions. You may end up spending too much time on one more time-consuming question, leaving insufficient time to answer the other less time-consuming questions. You may be able to answer one more time-consuming question correctly, but you could have utilized the same amount of time in answering five other less time-consuming questions. Remember, difficult questions are not always time-consuming; sometimes, an easy question can also be very time-consuming.

QUESTIONS ARRANGED FROM EASY TO HARD:

The questions on some of the sections of some of the standardized tests are arranged in the order of difficulty, i.e., they start from easy to hard, which means, the test begins with an easy question, and the level of difficulty of questions increases as you move along. If this is the case, you should start from the first question and try to move on in numeric order.

Note: This is typically true for math sections. The questions are almost never arranged from the easiest to the hardest in the critical reading or reading comprehension sections, in which a difficult question may be followed by an easier one.

DECIDE WHETHER TO DO IT NOW, GUESS, OR SKIP AND SAVE IT FOR LATER:

Think about the following while deciding when to answer the question:

(A) Do It Now: If this is the type of question you typically ace, and if you think you will be able to solve it easily and quickly – go ahead and answer it.

(B) Guess or Skip: If you think the question looks difficult or you normally don't do very well on such type of problems, and you don't have much confidence answering this particular type of question, or you are clueless, or you tried solving the problem and you are still stuck – don't waste your time, spend your time wisely by doing one of the following:

    (i) Guess: Eliminate any incorrect answer choices, make an educated guess from the remaining choices, and move on.

    (ii) Skip: Mark it in your test booklet so that you can come back to it later, and move on.

Note: Spend your time on the problems you can solve; if there's still time remaining at the end of the test – come back to the ones you had trouble with. It is better to get two points from two less challenging problems than spend the same amount of time on a tricky question you are unsure of.

You have limited time for each section, and each question is worth equal points, so it's very important to have an effective pacing strategy. Therefore:

$\Rightarrow$ Answer the easy questions first,
    $\Rightarrow$ then, deal with the moderately difficult questions,
        $\Rightarrow$ then at the end, tackle the difficult questions.

APPLY THE FOLLOWING LABELING SYSTEM FOR MOST EFFECTIVE USE:

Check Mark: "✓" $\Rightarrow$ Questions Answered
                                          $\Rightarrow$ Indicates you have answered the questions.

If you are on a question that you think is an easy question and you are confident that you can answer it correctly - simply solve it, put a check (✓) mark next to the question number after you answer it, and move on to the next question.

Double Check Mark: "✓✓" $\Rightarrow$ Answer Double Checked
                                          $\Rightarrow$ Indicates you have double checked the answer to the question.

If you are on a question that you have already answered but you are doubtful about the answer you chose and you decide to double check the answer to make sure that you have the correct answer - simply put a double check (✓✓) mark next to the question number after you answer it, and move on to the next question. If you realize that you had the incorrect answer the first time and now you have found the correct answer, make sure to change the answer choice on the answer sheet by completely erasing the old one and completely filling in the new answer choice.

Single Question Mark: "?" $\Rightarrow$ Moderately Difficult Questions
                                          $\Rightarrow$ Indicates the questions that you have tried but could not answer quickly, and you are capable of answering them and can possibly answer them with some more time and effort.

If you are on a question that you think is solvable but time consuming – you are still not getting anywhere, or you still are somewhat lost, but you think that with some more time you will be able to answer it correctly - skip the question and put a single question (?) mark next to it, so that you can come back to it later, if time permits. Also, make sure to leave the oval on the answer sheet blank to avoid marking answers to the wrong questions.

Double Question Mark: "??" $\Rightarrow$ Very Difficult Questions
                                          $\Rightarrow$ Indicates the questions that you have tried twice but could not answer, and it will be very difficult for you to answer them, and you may be able to answer them with a lot of time and effort.

If you are on a question that you think may be solvable but is very time consuming and difficult – you have already tried it twice, or you are not getting anywhere, or still lost, but you think that with a lot more time you may be able to answer it correctly - skip the question and put a double question (??) mark next to it, so that you can come back to it later, if time permits. Also, make sure to leave the oval on the answer sheet blank to avoid marking the answers to the wrong questions.

Cross Mark: "**x**"   ⇒ Questions Impossible to Answer
                                   ⇒ Indicates it is impossible for you to answer the question, and you are clueless or you don't even know where to start from.

If you are on a question that you think is impossible to answer – you are clueless about it or don't even know where to start from - skip the question and put a cross (**x**) mark next to it, so that you can come back to it later, if time permits. Also, make sure to leave the oval on the answer sheet blank to avoid marking answers to the wrong questions.

Blank Mark / Unmarked: "   "   ⇒ Not Yet Read/Attempted
                                   ⇒ Questions Not yet Read/Attempted. Indicates the questions that you have not even read or attempted.

If you have not yet been able to attempt the question – you have not even read the question - it means that question is not yet labeled and is unmarked.

ADVANTAGES OF QUESTION LABELING SYSTEM:

It is very important to label each question that you attempt. Following are some of the advantages of using our question labeling system:

- You will be able to identify questions you have answered.
- You will know which questions you have answered, and have double checked those answers.
- You will know which questions you have tried to answer but could not answer quickly, and you are capable of answering them and can possibly answer them with some more time and effort.
- You will know which questions you have tried to answer but could not answer, and it will be very difficult for you to answer them, and you may be able to answer them with a lot of time and effort.
- You will know which questions you have tried to answer and it is impossible for you to answer the questions, and you are clueless or don't even know where to start from.
- You will know which questions you have not yet attempted or answered.
- You will know which questions you should first go back to.
- You will know which questions you need to guess by using process of elimination strategy.
- You will easily get an idea of your progress throughout the test.
- Sometimes when you take a second look, a few hard questions may turn out to be simpler than how they looked the first time around.
- By first answering some easier questions, you can then come back to the harder questions with new eyes, a fresh perspective, and a newly acquired confidence.
- Sometimes answering another question may help you answer a question that you had skipped previously.

APPLY THE FOLLOWING PACING STRATEGY IN STRATEGIC ORDER:

FIRST ROUND: ANSWER THE EASY QUESTIONS:

In the first round, make a quick initial pass through the entire section answering all the easy questions, the questions that you think you can answer with very little time and thinking - you should try to answer these questions directly without using the process of elimination strategy and guessing. As you solve these questions, put a check mark (✓) on them so that you know you have answered them. Also, make sure to fill in the corresponding ovals on your answer sheet.

SECOND ROUND: ANSWER THE MODERATE QUESTIONS:

After you've browsed through every question in the section and answered or guessed the questions which seem easiest to you, go back to the moderately difficult questions that have a single question (?) mark next to them - depending on how much time you are left with, if you are still not able to answer them correctly - use the process of elimination strategy discussed later in this book and make an educated guess. As you solve these questions, put check marks on them so that you know you have answered them. Also make sure to fill in the corresponding ovals on your answer sheet.

THIRD ROUND: ANSWER THE DIFFICULT QUESTIONS:

After answering all the easy questions and the moderate questions with a single question mark, go back to the difficult questions that have a double question (??) mark next to them - depending on how much time you are left with, if you are still clueless and still don't know where to start from - use the process of elimination strategy discussed later in this book and try to eliminate at least one answer choice and then make an educated guess. As you solve these questions, put a check mark on them so that you know you have answered them. Also, make sure to fill in the corresponding ovals on your answer sheet.

FOURTH ROUND: ANSWER ANY REMAINING QUESTIONS:

During the last 2-3 minutes of the test, use the process of elimination strategy to the maximum and try to answer any remaining questions by making educated guesses. As you solve these questions, put a check mark on them so that you know you have answered them. Also, make sure to fill in the corresponding ovals on your answer sheet.

FIFTH ROUND: DOUBLE-CHECK YOUR ANSWERS:

After completing the first four rounds, if you realize that you have answered all the questions and you still have time remaining - you should not waste that time by sitting idle, instead you should invest that time in double checking your answers.

- If you find any mistakes and realize that your answer was incorrect – make sure you get the correct answer this time and put a double checkmark next to the question.
- If you are unsure of some of your answers – go back and reconsider them. Also, make sure to completely erase your old answers and fill in the corresponding ovals on your answer sheet.

Make sure that you recorded your answers correctly.

Note: Please note that you can apply this step after finishing all the easy and moderate questions and before even attempting the difficult questions. The advantage of doing this is you will be making sure that you get the easy and moderate questions correct by double checking your answers, before even trying to attempt the difficult questions, which you are not at all sure about.

MINIMIZE THE NUMBER OF QUESTION MARKS:

Skipping or jumping around all over the test can result in waste of some very valuable time. You should briefly read the question for the first time and decide in the first few seconds whether you are capable of answering it or not. If you don't feel too comfortable with the question, just mark that question with a question mark and don't waste too much of your time trying to answer it. You should try to minimize the number of question marks on your test booklet to no more than 10% of the test. Otherwise, you will have to spend double the time re-reading these questions when you come back to them.

THINGS TO NOTE ABOUT PACING:

- It's normal to see some questions that you think are very difficult. Instead of tackling them in your first round, skip them and mark them appropriately so that you can come back to them later.
- Don't ponder too much on any one question until you've laid eyes on every question at least once.
- Towards the end of a section, if you find yourself running out of time, start locating and answering the questions that can earn you quick and easy points.
- Make sure to leave some extra time towards the end of each section so you can make sure you have answered all the questions and have some time to review your work.

10.4: HOW TO MARK ANSWERS:

Before you take the test, you must become familiar with the test booklet, answer document, and scratch paper. Knowing this in advance will save you time and worry when you take the actual test.

SCRATCH PAPER:

(A) Test Booklet: Your test booklet serves as your scratch paper; you are allowed to write whatever you want, wherever you want in the section of the test booklet that you are working on.

(B) Answer Sheet: Do not use the answer sheet as scratch paper; you are only allowed to mark your answers in the answer sheet. So keep the answer sheet neat and free of any kind of stray marks.

USE YOUR TEST BOOKLET TO MAKE NOTES:

- Work out calculations.
- When a question contains a figure, note any given measurements or the values you calculate right on the figure in the test booklet.
- Mark each question that you don't answer so that you can easily go back to it later.
- When working on a question, cross out each answer choice you eliminate.
- As you read each question, circle what's been asked so that you can be sure you are answering the right question.

MARKING ANSWERS ON THE ANSWER SHEET:

(A) Make sure you Mark your Answers on the Answer Sheet: You will not receive any credit for anything written in the test booklet. So make sure that you mark your answers on the answer sheet.

(B) Mark Only One Answer for Each Question: If you mark more than one answer for any question, you will not get any credit, even if one of the choices that you marked was the correct answer. If the machine reads two answers for the same question, it will mark the question wrong. So make sure that you mark only one answer for each question.

(C) No Credit will be Given for Answers Marked in the Test Booklet: If you mark your answer in the test booklet and not on the answer sheet, you will not get any credit, even if you have the correct answer and marked it in the test booklet. You will not get the credit for answering it correctly unless you mark the correct answer at the appropriate spot on the answer sheet. So make sure that you mark your answer on the answer sheet to get credit for answering it correctly.

MARKING ANSWERS IN THE RIGHT SPOT:

Make sure that the answer oval you are marking on the answer sheet corresponds to the number of the question in the test booklet. Each numbered row will contain five ovals corresponding to each answer choice for that question. Fill in the oval on the answer sheet which corresponds to your answer choice in the test booklet. When marking a response on the answer sheet, it's very important that you make sure that you are marking it in the proper space.

(A) Mismarking can Throw off your Entire Score: If you mismark even one answer, or inadvertently skip a line or lose your place on the answer sheet, it can lead you to marking all of your subsequent answers in the wrong spots, and that can throw off your entire score.

(B) Periodic Checks: Periodically, check to make sure that you have not unintentionally left a blank space, or filled in two answer choices in the same column for a single question. Always double check to make sure that you marked the answers in the right spots. After every few questions, check to make sure that the number of the question in the test booklet corresponds with the number on the answer sheet. Every five questions or so, it is a good idea to take a look at the number in the test booklet and the number on your answer key to insure they match. Also, check them carefully every time you skip a question.

Note: Since the multiple choice sections are graded by a machine, even if you get the correct answer and mark it in the wrong spot, it would be impossible for the machine to know that, and therefore, no credit will be given.

LEAVE THE OVAL BLANK FOR SKIPPED QUESTIONS:

If you skip a question due to any reason, circle the question you skip so that you can easily locate it later. Also, make sure that you leave the corresponding oval on the answer sheet blank to avoid marking answers at the wrong spots for all the subsequent questions.

FILL IN THE OVALS COMPLETELY, DARKLY AND NEATLY:

(A) Fill in the Ovals Completely, Darkly, and Neatly: Since the multiple choice sections are scored by a machine, make sure to fill in the ovals completely, darkly, and neatly using a number 2 pencil. Since there are no humans involved, it would be almost impossible for the machine to detect any errors.

(B) Do not Overflow the Ovals: Overflowing the ovals on the answer sheet can mislead the scoring machine and make it pick the incorrect answer choice or even disqualify that question from the scoring process. So be very careful, and do not overflow the ovals on the answer sheet by making exceedingly large marks on your answer sheet.

(C) Do not Make any Stray Marks on your Answer Sheet: Stray marks on the answer sheet can also mislead the scoring machine and make it pick the incorrect answer choice or even disqualify that question from the scoring process. So be very careful, and do not make any stray marks on the answer sheet.

(D) If you Change your Answer, the Old one must be Removed Completely: You may change your answers on the answer sheet, but remember to erase the old answer completely. This is very important, because the answer sheets are machine scored, partly erased marks could cause the machine to score your answer incorrectly, since a machine can't distinguish between a stray mark, accidental mark, and an actually filled-in answer.

FILL IN THE ANSWERS ON YOUR ANSWER SHEET IN BLOCKS:

Enter your answers on your answer sheet in blocks to save valuable time. It is recommended that you fill in the answers on your answer sheet in blocks of four to five answers at a time. As you start answering questions, simply circle the correct answers in your test question booklet. After you have finished answering four to five questions, transfer those answers on to your answer sheet. This method of marking your answers onto your answer sheet in blocks is more efficient then moving back and forth between your test question booklet and answer sheet after answering each question. Applying this technique of filling in the answers on your answer sheet in blocks will not only result in saving some very valuable time, but will also ensure filling in your answers in the correct spot. This technique may be particularly useful in the reading comprehension section, where it is very important not to be interrupted by a break of link in your chain of thoughts while comprehending the passage.

Be Careful during the Last Few Minutes: If you are applying this technique of filling in the answers onto your answer sheet in blocks, be very careful when you approach the last two to three minutes of each section. When you reach the last two to three minutes of each section, enter your answers as you answer them. It would be a shame to be left with a block of questions that you have answered but not being able to enter them on the answer sheet before the time is up for that section. You may not fill in answers on your answer document after the time is up.

HORIZONTAL OR VERTICAL ANSWER KEYS:

Also pay attention to find out whether the answer key numbers are horizontal or vertical. Otherwise, you may end up marking your answers to the questions on the wrong spots, and that can cost you the whole test.

CHECK YOUR ANSWER GRID:

If you mark all the answers and happen to have some extra time left over at the end of the test, it would be a perfect time to look over each question and make sure that you marked the answers on your answer sheet (or on the computer screen) in the right spots. If you did make any errors in marking, you'd be able to catch and correct them before it's too late.

WRITING RESPONSE FOR WRITING SECTION:

For the writing section, write legibly or type accurately in English in the correct place on the answer document or on the computer screen. The readers must be able to easily read what you have written, or else they will not be able to score your essay fairly. It's not a hand writing competition, but it won't hurt to write neatly, or at the least, you must write legibly. You must write your essay using a soft-lead pencil and not a mechanical pencil. If you make corrections, do so very thoroughly and cleanly. You may write corrections or additions neatly between the lines, but you may not write in the margins.

PART 11.0: CAREER MANAGEMENT PLAN:

TABLE OF CONTENTS:

THIS PAGE HAS BEEN INTENTIONALLY LEFT BLANK.

11.1: COLLEGE APPLICATION:

REASONS TO GET HIGHER EDUCATION:
Here are a few good reasons why you should get higher education:

- Higher education is increasingly becoming more and more important for the current generation than it was for previous generations. Today, we live in a world which is highly competitive. In order to compete and rise in this new era, it's imperative that you obtain a little bit more than just basic education. Most corporations want to hire people who are highly educated and skilled.
- Higher education and skill level is directly proportional to high paying jobs. Most college graduates earn a much higher salary than people with just high school diplomas, and most post graduates earn significantly more than just college graduates.
- The higher the level of your education, the more likely it is that you will have a more stable and secure job.
- Higher education also comes with a lot of other benefits, such as polishing your overall personality, developing good communication skills, and most importantly, experiencing success.

TOP 10 COLLEGE APPLICATION MISTAKES:
Following are the top ten college application mistakes:

#1: Spellings and Grammatical Errors: You must make every effort to make your college application forms free from any sort of spelling and grammatical errors. If you misspell or make a grammatical error on something as important as the application, it means that either you are careless or aren't good at spelling and grammar. Don't rely completely on the word processors spell/grammar check as there are many errors that the software can't catch. Make sure to manually proofread for spelling and grammatical errors.

#2: Writing Illegibly: You must pen in your best handwriting if you are filling out hard copies of application forms. Even though colleges are not going to accept or reject you for your handwriting skills, still first impressions count. Your application is often your first contact with the colleges. Also, make sure that the application form has only one style of handwriting throughout the form. It's okay to get help from someone to fill the application form but there is no reason to transfer this information to the colleges. Hence, take your time and use your best handwriting as it will help you make a better impression.

#3: Missing Fields: Make sure to complete all required fields and not to leave anything blank on all pages of the form. Even if there are optional fields, you must try to fill them as this is a good opportunity for you to say more about yourself. Incomplete application forms, especially without your signature and date, may be returned to you and the fees may not be refunded.

#4: Wrong Information: Make sure to read the application forms carefully and fill in correct information at the correct spot. For instance, if the form asks for your date of birth, make sure to enter it in the format asked, such as month/date/year or date/month/year.

#5: Whacky Email Address: This may sound silly to you but sometimes small things make big impressions. Using a whacky email address (such as, PunkStar77@xyz.com) may be a good fun idea with your friends, but not with colleges. Keep your fun address for friends, but select a professional email address (such as John.Smith@xyz.com), preferably with your first and/or last name with no kicks for college and job applications.

#6: Not Checking the Correspondence: If the colleges have any questions or need further information from you, they will contact you via email or regular mail. Make sure to regularly check your mails so that you can promptly send your reply. You don't want to miss out on any important correspondence related to your college application process.

#7: Application Not Submitted: If you are applying online, make sure to receive a confirmation that the college or university received it. This confirmation could be an email message or a webpage displaying the confirmation. You may also receive a confirmation via regular mail. Follow up and make sure that your application has been submitted and received by the colleges.

#8: Transcript Errors: Make sure to review your transcripts before sending them to colleges as they may sometimes have errors. In most circumstances, you'll have to send your transcripts directly from your school for an additional fee.

#9: False Information: Make sure to give true information about yourself. For instance, if you enter that you won the county championship for tennis, make sure that this is true and not fabricated information.

#10: Application Archive: Finally, don't forget to keep a copy of all your application material.

11.2: COLLEGE ADMISSION:

PLAN YOUR COURSE SELECTION:

Colleges give importance to which courses you're taking or have taken previously. It tells colleges what kind of goals you have and what kind of academic career you are more inclined towards. Colleges are usually more impressed by decent grades in challenging courses than by outstanding grades in easy ones. For instance, getting a "B" in a course related to an advanced calculus course will be much more impressive than an "A" in a fine arts course, especially if you plan to apply to engineering colleges. Hence, make sure to try to sign up for advanced and honors classes, and pick electives that really stretch your mind and help you develop new skills.

TOP FIVE COLLEGE ADMISSION CRITERIA:

The admission process at each college/university is unique. Each college will have different requirements, prerequisites, and levels of selectivity. While some specific requirements vary, every college/university sets some basic standards for evaluating prospective students, such as the ones given below, in the order of importance:

(A) GPA: GPA is computed by multiplying the number of grade points earned in each course (generally, A=4, B=3, C=2, D=1, F=0) by the number of course/credit hours, then dividing the sum by the total number of course/credit hours taken. Class rank is a rating that compares your cumulative GPA to other members of your class. Class rank is often used as a college admission and scholarship standard. A high GPA is an important criterion for college admission; however, it's not the only thing college recruiters are looking for in prospective students. One of the things admission officers pay attention to, besides GPA, is the kind of classes you have taken previously. Moreover, most colleges look at the courses you have taken before in order to decide which courses you will be allowed to take.

(B) Standardized Test Scores: Besides your GPA, most colleges look at your national standardized test scores. Your standardized score, together with your GPA, indicates how prepared you are for college and the program of your choice.

(C) Letters of Recommendation: Most college applications require at least one letter of recommendation from your past instructor and/or employer. They want to hear from someone who has taught you or under whom you have worked previously. Make sure that the person writing your letter of recommendation thinks favorably about you. Give your references plenty of time and don't try to rush them if you want them to write you a glorious letter of recommendation.

(D) Essays: Most college applications require at least one essay, so spend time and try to write an outstanding essay. It's okay to get some outside help and get ideas from the internet, but at the end, your essay should represent your own thoughts and opinions. In fact, this is your first chance to say whatever you want to communicate about yourself to the admission officer. So make your case and put your best foot forward.

(E) Interviews: Once a college is satisfied with all the other pieces of your application, they may require a personal interview or examples of work in special areas such as art or music. Be prepared to interview, audition, or submit a portfolio, if you are asked.

IMPORTANCE OF EACH ADMISSION CRITERION:

The standardized test score is only one of several factors examined by admission officers. In addition to a good standardized test score, schools normally also consider many other aspects of an application before making an admission decision, such as high school/undergraduate GPA, work experience, letters of recommendation, essays, interviews, etc.

However, it needs to be noted that your standardized test scores and the GPA are the most important criteria in making an admission decision. The letters of recommendation and essays can help you but they wouldn't be the ultimate deciding factors. These are only additional supporting requirements, which may help the colleges decide how likely you are to fit into their campus community and to succeed in their academic program. No matter how awesome your essay is, it won't get you into college if you don't meet the other academic requirements. However, if you have been short listed as one of the probable candidates, the essay can possibly push you higher up in the list.

For instance, students who obtain a score below some required average standardized test score may still be able to make up for this by some other means, such as, an excellent undergraduate GPA or by writing a remarkable essay as part of the application process. Moreover, as surprising as it may seem, in some cases, doing well in the personal interview with an admission officer or other university representative may be just as, or even more important. So, although scoring high on the standardized test should be a desired goal and it must be pursued with all the means possible, it is by no means the only requirement for admission to a school.

Different schools pay different weight to different admission factors in their final admission decision. Before applying to a college or university, figure out what criteria are considered for admission and how these criteria are ranked by order of importance. Regardless of your standardized test score, you should contact the schools of your choice to learn more about them, and to ask about how they use standardized test scores and other admission criteria (such as your undergraduate grades, essays, and letters of recommendation) to evaluate applicants for admission.

Every university and college requiring the standardized test sets their own requirements. You may have to do some research to find the minimum standardized test score requirement of specific schools where you intend to apply for admission. A good source to find this information is the school websites, admission officers and advisors, college catalogs, and materials published by the school. Some do, but most college catalogs do not explicitly state what their minimum standardized test requirement is; however, the annual reports of most schools do mention the average standardized test score of the last incoming student body or the last batch of graduating students.

Therefore, a low standardized test score does not necessarily mean that no university/college will accept you, nor does a high standardized test score guarantee acceptance at the school of your choice. Nevertheless, since the standardized test score is one of the most important factors, you should make an effort to do as well as you can on the test. Following the advice given in this book and going through our other modules will ensure that you maximize your score.

Standardized test scores may also be considered a major factor in determining the eligibility for financial aid. Contact the specific school for more accurate admission requirements. However, make sure if it is a minimum or an average figure.

Minimum vs. Average Score Requirement:
(A) If it is a minimum score requirement, then all it means is that this is the cut-off mark, that is, your application will not even be considered if your score is below this figure. By the same token, meeting this minimum score requirement does not ensure your admission either. Therefore, this minimum score requirement is just a good indication of the necessary approximate figure for admission.

(B) If it is an average score, then it is just an average score requirement without any cut-off. Getting a score little below that figure does not mean that acceptance is not possible; there may be some who scored lower than this figure and still get accepted. Likewise, getting a score little above that figure does not mean that acceptance is guaranteed; there may be some who scored more than this figure and still got rejected. After all, this is just an average score.

SCALED SCORES & PERCENTILE RANKS:
In addition to scaled scores, you will also receive a percentile rank, which will place your performance relative to those of a large sample population of other test takers. The percentile rank shows what percent of test takers scored at or below your score level. For instance, a percentile rank of 85 means that 85 percent did as well or worse than you did and that only 15 percent did better than you.

Since the test is graded on a predetermined curve, the scaled score corresponds to a certain percentile rank, which will also be given on your score report. For instance, an 80th percentile, meaning that 80 percent of test takers scored at or below this level and 20 percent of test takers scored above this level.

The sample population that you are compared against in order to determine your percentile is not everyone else who takes the test the same day or same location as you do. The test administrator wants to be as fair as possible, and do not want to penalize an unlucky candidate who takes the test at a time when everyone else happens to have above avergae intelligence, or reward a lucky candidate who takes the test at a time when everyone else happens to have below average intelligence. Therefore, your score will not at all be affected by the other people who take the test on the same day as you; instead, they compare your performance with those of a random three-year population of recent test-takers.

Percentile scores tell schools just what your scaled scores are worth. So the percentile figure is important because it allows admission officers at business schools to quickly get a sense of where you fall among other applicants. For instance, even if everyone gets a very high scaled score, universities would still be able to differentiate candidates by their percentile score.

Percentile ranks match with scaled scores differently, depending on the measure. For instance, if you were to get a perfect score in each section, it would translate into different percentile ranks. In Verbal you'd be scoring above 99 percent of the population, so that would be your percentile rank. But in the Quantitative section, many other people will score very high as well. Many people score so well on it that high scaled scores are not that difficult. Your percentile rank for Quantitative section would only be in the 96th percentile. The reason being that so many other people have scored so high in quantitative section that no one can score above the 96th percentile. With this, we can conclude that it's comparatively easier to get good scaled scores and much harder to get good percentile ranks. The relative frequency of high scaled scores means that universities pay great attention to percentile ranks.

It would be a good idea to do some real research into the programs and schools you're interested in. Many schools have cut-off scores below which they don't even consider applicants. But be aware, the cut-off score is just a baseline below which they won't even consider your application, and merely getting a score that meets that baseline doesn't guarantee your admission.

MAKE THE FINAL DECISION:

Although waiting for notices of college acceptances can be agonizing, once admission notices are received, the decision-making process begins. Make your decision carefully and thoughtfully, and accept an offer that's the right match for you. In case your dream college doesn't accept you, don't be disheartened, maybe that college wasn't going to be good for you. A college education is an important and valuable investment in your future, regardless of where you get it from. As soon as you make your final decision, inform the school that you have accepted their offer, and don't forget to let all the other schools who have extended offers to you know of your decision as well.

First decide on the kind of program you are most interested in. Use your skills, interests, and preferences as the basis of choosing a college program. Once you decide which program interests you the most, it's time to decide which college to go to. Remember, a decision about college is a big part of your overall long-term career planning process. Decide what you want to achieve in life and use your college as a bridge to help you get there. For example, if you are fascinated by sculptures and wish to make a career in it, look for a good arts school.

Following are some of the important things to consider while evaluating and comparing colleges:
(A) **Location:** distance from home, climate, etc.
(B) **Environment:** type of school (public or private), school setting (urban, rural), location & size of nearest city, co-ed, male, female, religious affiliations, etc.
(C) **Size:** enrollment, physical size of campus, etc.
(D) **Admission requirements:** deadline(s), tests required, average test scores, GPA, rank, special requirements, etc.
(E) **Academics:** programs offered, special requirements, accreditation, student-faculty ratio, typical class size, etc.
(F) **Cost:** total cost of tuition, books, supplies, etc.
(G) **Financial aid:** deadline(s), required forms, percent of student population receiving aid, scholarships, part-time employment opportunities, etc.
(H) **College expenses:** tuition, room & board, estimated total budget, application fee, deposits, etc.
(I) **Housing:** residence hall requirements, availability, types and sizes, food plans, etc.
(J) **Facilities:** Academic, recreational, etc.
(K) **Social Activities:** clubs, organizations, sororities/fraternities, athletics, intramurals, etc.
(L) **Job Prospects:** area recruiters, average starting salary of fresh graduates, etc.
Sources of information: College catalogs, information bulletins, college representatives, college fairs, school counselors and teachers, other professionals in the field, students and alumni, college websites, etc.

THE COST OF EDUCATION:

Before you make your final decision in selecting one of the colleges who have accepted you, it'll be a good idea to figure out how much it will cost and how you intend to pay for it. The cost of education includes:
- tuition and fees
- room and board
- books and supplies
- transportation
- other personal expenses

FINANCIAL AID:

Financial aid is a general term used for any financial assistance given to a student for any type of postsecondary education. Every college has a financial aid office, which can provide more information on how you can get financial aid and who would qualify for it. There are several types of financial aid and a variety of sources of financial assistance. Generally, financial aid is divided into two groups: need-based financial aid and merit-based financial aid. However, some special type of financial aid is based on academic performance or selective skills.

CAREER PLANNING TIPS:

Explore your career options because choosing or planning a career is a big decision. This is not a one time process; you'll be continuously planning for your career and making changes as and when needed. Career planning is a step-by-step process which you will go through repeatedly throughout your lifetime. You must know your strengths and look for your options, and then determine what it will take to reach your goals.

Apply the following process to make the right career decisions.

First: Take an honest and realistic look at yourself.
Consider the following points:
- Know what yours strengths are.
- Know what your weaknesses are.
- Think about the areas of your interest.
- Think about your ambitions and goals.

Next: Explore your options.
Consider the following points:
- Be aware of the possibilities.
- Talk to your counselor, colleagues, family, and friends.
- Volunteer or work in a job that interests you.
- Research about your interest on the internet, books, magazines, etc.

Finally: Find the best fit between your goals and the options available to you.
Consider the following points:
- Which schools offer the programs you are most interested in?
- How will you pay for your education?
- Will you be able to find your dream job?
- How will you manage your other personal and social commitments?

THIS PAGE HAS BEEN INTENTIONALLY LEFT BLANK.

NOTES:

NOTES:

NOTES:

NOTES:

NOTES:

NOTES:

NOTES:

NOTES:

NOTES:

NOTES:

NOTES:

NOTES:

NOTES:

NOTES:

EZ BOOK STORE: ORDERS & SALES:

ORDERS & SALES INFORMATION: EZ Solutions books can be ordered via one of the following methods:

⌨ ON-LINE ORDERS:
On-line Orders can be placed 24/7 via internet by going to: www.EZmethods.com

✉ E-MAIL ORDERS:
E-Mail Orders can be placed 24/7 via internet by emailing: orders@EZmethods.com

☎ PHONE ORDERS:
Phone Orders can be placed via telephone by calling: ++301.622.9597

▭ FAX ORDERS:
Fax Orders can be placed via fax by faxing: ++301.622.9597

▤ MAIL ORDERS:
Mail Orders can be placed via regular mail by mailing to the address given below:
EZ Solutions
Orders Department
P.O. Box 10755
Silver Spring, MD 20914
USA

OTHER OPTIONS: EZ Solutions books are also available at most major bookstores.

Institutional Sales: For volume/bulk sales to bookstores, libraries, schools, colleges, universities, organization, and institutions, please contact us. Quantity discount and special pricing is available.

EZ Book List:

List of EZ Test Prep Series of Books:

EZ Test Prep Series books are available for the following sections:
- EZ Solutions – Test Prep Series – General – Test Taker's Manual
- EZ Solutions – Test Prep Series – Math Strategies
- EZ Solutions – Test Prep Series – Math Review – Arithmetic
- EZ Solutions – Test Prep Series – Math Review – Algebra
- EZ Solutions – Test Prep Series – Math Review – Applications
- EZ Solutions – Test Prep Series – Math Review – Geometry
- EZ Solutions – Test Prep Series – Math Review – Word Problems
- EZ Solutions – Test Prep Series – Math Review – Logic & Stats
- EZ Solutions – Test Prep Series – Math Practice – Basic Workbook
- EZ Solutions – Test Prep Series – Math Practice – Advanced Workbook
- EZ Solutions – Test Prep Series – Verbal Section – Reading Comprehension
- EZ Solutions – Test Prep Series – Verbal Section – Sentence Correction/Completion
- EZ Solutions – Test Prep Series – Verbal Section – Critical Reasoning
- EZ Solutions – Test Prep Series – Verbal Section – Vocabulary
- EZ Solutions – Test Prep Series – Verbal Section – Grammar
- EZ Solutions – Test Prep Series – Verbal Section – Writing Skills

Note: Some of these books have already been published and others will be released shortly.

EZ Test Prep Series books are available for the following standardized tests:
- EZ Solutions GMAT Test Prep Series of Books
- EZ Solutions GRE Test Prep Series of Books
- EZ Solutions SAT Test Prep Series of Books
- EZ Solutions ACT Test Prep Series of Books
- EZ Solutions PRAXIS Test Prep Series of Books
- EZ Solutions POWER MATH Test Prep Series of Books